T0386778

OUT OF THE DARKNESS

OUT OF THE DARKNESS

Greenham Voices
1981–2000

KATE KERROW & REBECCA MORDAN

The
History
Press

For Greenham Women Everywhere,
and in memory of Marie Knowles and her anarchist heart

First published 2021

The History Press
97 St George's Place, Cheltenham,
Gloucestershire, GL50 3QB
www.thehistorypress.co.uk

British Library Cataloguing in Publication Data.
A catalogue record for this book is available from the British Library.

ISBN 978 0 7509 9517 7

Typesetting and origination by The History Press
Printed and bound in Great Britain by TJ Books Limited, Padstow, Cornwall.

Trees for LYfe

CONTENTS

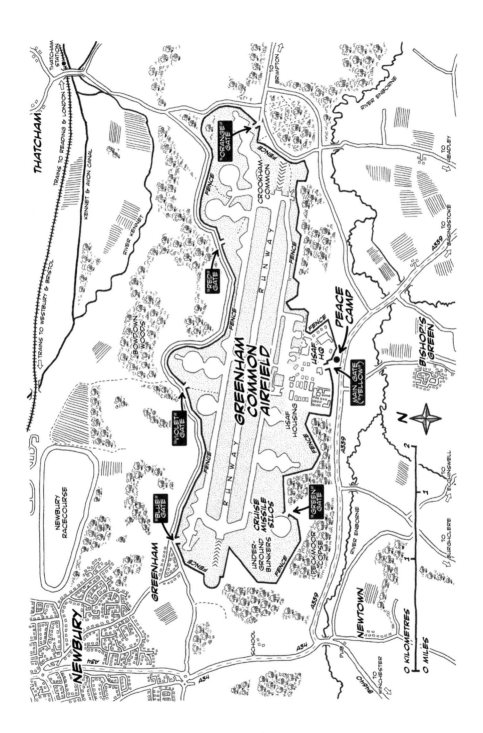

FOREWORD

Dear contributors and readers,

I am so, so honoured to be writing this foreword, to be a part of telling the stories of the women who participated in the extraordinary time that was Greenham. I am especially honoured that the name of one of my songs is being used as the title of this unique book.

I consider myself to have been a back-row Greenham woman. I never camped there and only visited to sing and be hauled around by police on a couple of occasions. I had been singing about women, war and peace, injustice and inequality for many years. In 1968, while researching songs with Peggy Seeger and Sandra Kerr to tour folk clubs and make an album of women's songs, I began to wake up to how traditional songs could illuminate the lives of our women ancestors and how songs could be an act of transgression and resistance. This in turn led to working with Kathy Henderson and Sandra on *My Song is My Own: 100 Women's Songs* in 1972. By then we had a stronger understanding of the nature of patriarchy and how it seeped into every facet of our society. The environmental destruction was already evident, and the warmongering led to the formation of Women for Life on Earth, which I joined at its outset in London, where I lived at the time. We recognised that patriarchy and militarism were inextricable and that, in our name, the government had invited US nuclear warheads on to our green and pleasant land.

Then the Cardiff Women for Life on Earth began that legendary walk. I remember receiving the photocopied newsletter telling us that a group from Wales, primarily women, were planning to set off for Greenham Common where the missiles were due to be posted. My contribution has always been to sing and sing with others, so that's what I did to help. Standing up for my beliefs and simply singing them through the depth, power, beauty, rage and tenderness of the naked voice was an act of resistance, hoping to move hearts and heads and inspire them to change what needed changing.

And then came the Women – with a capital W. Hundreds and thousands of us, surrounding the base and decorating the fence with wonderful, wild, gentle mementos. The 9-mile perimeter fence was transformed into a living collage describing women's powerful commitment to peace. Women of all ages, nationalities and races were willing to stand with that same power and energy, to put our lives on the line, to go to prison and to fill the courtrooms with song. Songs were everywhere all the time. We sang and I sang, so glad to be of use, to lend my voice at rallies, benefit concerts, meetings and voice workshops, and to write songs to trumpet the doomsday threat of nuclear annihilation.

This book tells of women raising their voices. It documents the bravery, hardships, camaraderie, determination and dedication of women who spent time at the Greenham camp. Forty years have elapsed since that momentous walk, and it is more necessary than ever that these stories reach a wider public. Greenham laid the foundations for so many of the recent courageous and imaginative protests and actions against militarism and environmental disaster.

I dedicate this foreword to one of my sisters in song: Peggy Seeger was a mentor for me in the 1960s and will be a source of inspiration during the rest of my days. Together we encourage you to use this book to bring hope, passion and song to the struggles that are coming to save this beautiful earth and all her creatures. I can do no better than quote Peggy's song 'Carry Greenham Home' here:

Help to save the world we love,
Velvet fist in iron glove

Frankie Armstrong
(with Peggy Seeger)
June 2021

PREFACE

KATE KERROW AND REBECCA MORDAN

This book, which is about one of the most successful examples of collective female activism in history, also originated in female activism and collaboration. Firstly, the collaboration of two friends over an idea, then the united energies of a dedicated team of women interviewers who aided the collation of the Greenham women's stories, and finally, the efforts of a feminist publishing director committed to bringing this research and the impactful history of the Greenham Common Women's Peace Camp to print.

Our work has always been rooted in the research, documentation and artistic celebration of women's stories. We both had a long-term fascination with the women of Greenham and Rebecca had been a Greenham child who Embraced the Base with her mother and 30,000 other women and girls in 1982. Sadly, we became increasingly aware that, whenever we spoke to people younger than us, they had rarely heard of Greenham.

Women from all over the UK, and the world, had braved every weather and indignity to live together and protest peacefully and creatively about the threat to humankind from the nuclear arms race. Before the internet and mobile phones, the women and their supporters managed to organise non-violent protest groups tens of thousands in size. And yet, the staggering fortitude of the women who lived at the camp full time, despite bailiffs and police destroying their property and often violently removing them from the site, was apparently unworthy of robust historical documentation.

Despite being largely undiscussed and unapplauded now, the women's peace camp made a huge impact at the time. It inspired similar movements all around the world, including in the USA and Russia. The women were developing the tactics of non-violent direct action (NVDA) from luminaries like the Ladies' Land League in Ireland, Gandhi, the Civil Rights movement and American disability rights activists. Using

A peace sign being painted on Ginnie Evans's face by Sue Bolton; they then joined an action dressed as witches and cut down hundreds of yards of fence. (Bridget Boudewijn)

these strategies, the women were able to remain on a site from which authorities repeatedly tried to remove them – suffering repeated arrests, police and military harassment, and a lack of facilities like toilets or electricity – eventually growing their presence to a camp that thousands of protestors flocked to during its nineteen-year existence.

By 1991, the last missiles were being removed from the base and, by 1992, RAF Greenham Common was out of operation. Additionally, thanks to the efforts of a final group of women who remained at the camp after the cruise missiles left, the common was taken off the military and given back to the people in 2000.[1]

To address the problematic suppression of such important history, with the support of the Heritage Lottery Fund, we decided to gather what would become the largest collection of Greenham stories, first hand, from the women themselves, so as to preserve their history in their own words, and to celebrate their actions, trials, troubles and achievements.

We trained fifteen remarkable women as interviewers, sourced from all over the UK, with ages ranging from 18 to 80. Between them, they represented women who were at work, pregnant, bringing up children, running businesses and arts hubs, studying or teaching, in retirement, in academia, and women who had been at Greenham themselves. We worked with the Women's Library at the London School of Economics, Falmouth Film School, the University of the West of England, the Feminist Library, the Hypatia Trust and Kresen Kernow to best capture and archive these testimonies. Sisterly bodies like Dreadnought South West and the Vote 100 campaign spread the news of our project to their followers and, through all our partners, word carried. As a result we were able to collate over 100 Greenham women's voices into an archive entitled *Greenham Women Everywhere*, which comprises over 200 hours of long-form, previously unheard audio.

In this book we centre the fascinating testimonies we've collected, using the women's own words to bring the camp to life. It is intended as an anecdotal history of the peace camp; the interviews we collected are shaped by memory, personal opinion and experience. The camp existed for almost two decades and many thousands of individual women have had personal experiences of it. As such, the aim of the book is to reveal their stories in their words, and not to establish and contain the history to one official and definite truth. But we do aim to show the astounding strategy and bravery behind the Greenham campaign, and reveal just how much we owe to these fearless campaigners.

THE WOMEN IN THIS BOOK

ALISON NAPIER

Alison was a sociology student in Aberdeen when she was asked by some friends if she would drive a minibus for them down to Greenham. She visited many times afterwards and was involved in many actions at the camp.

ANN PETTITT AND KARMEN THOMAS

Believing women's voices needed to be heard in the male-dominated world of politics and anti-nuclear movements, Ann Pettitt and Karmen Thomas initiated the 1981 Women for Life on Earth walk from Cardiff to Greenham Common US Air Force/RAF base. Their aim was to initiate a public debate with the government regarding nuclear weapons, in particular cruise missiles, to engage the media and make the topic known in every household.

ANNE SCARGILL

Anne Scargill visited Greenham in solidarity, having been made aware of the camp by her then-husband Arthur. She was a key part of Women Against Pit Closures, a huge campaign made up mainly of working-class women from coalfield communities who were protesting against the Thatcher government's policy of closing British pits.

ANNEI SOANES

Annei went to Greenham after getting involved in her local CND movement. She was working at Harrods at the time. The day after participating in an NVDA workshop, she resigned and began her life working for peace.

ANNIE BROTHERTON

In 1984 Annie and her girlfriend decided to visit Greenham for a night; there she became aware of police violence. The experience made her want to contribute, so the pair came back to live at Blue Gate.

BECKY GRIFFITHS

Becky first went to Greenham for the Embrace the Base action when she was 17 years old. She moved to Greenham soon after and lived at Yellow Gate full time for over two years. With others, including her mother Naomi, she helped free the geese the military were using to guard the Greenham nuclear airbase.

BETTY LEVENE

Betty was very involved in the peace movement and anti-nuclear campaigns before going to Greenham in 1981. She has remained active in the peace movement all her life.

BRIDGET BOUDEWIJN

Bridget visited the camp many times, bringing the ethos of NVDA back to her local protests. She created photography and art of the actions she was involved with, including those at Greenham.

CAROLYN FRANCIS

Carolyn was at Green Gate in summer 1984. After leaving college and travelling the wilds of Canada, she stayed at Greenham's London base where she supported herself by busking, and then moved to the camp to provide music there. Her sister Sally and her mum also protested at the base. Carolyn's time at Green Gate led her to Buddism and she teaches, composes and performs on a variety of instruments, including the fiddle and pipes.

ELIZABETH BEECH

Elizabeth took a bus to Embrace the Base in 1982 with a Glastonbury women's group. She lived at Yellow Gate from 1983 to 1987. Her time at Greenham lost her the custody of her two children; the trial was seen by many as a political strategy to frighten mothers at the camp into going home.

ELIZABETH GREENLAND

Elizabeth's time at Greenham was often spent with her young children and other families there. Having seen the camp's impact on the peace movement as a whole, Elizabeth works with her local Extinction Rebellion to pass on the women's campaigning methods.

ELIZABETH WOODCRAFT

Elizabeth represented the Greenham women at their hearings at Newbury Magistrates Court. She is the author of various novels including *The Girls from Greenway*.

FENJA HILL

Originally from a military family, Fenja is honest about her reasons for coming to camp not being at all political – initially at least. However, she is clear that the legacy of Greenham has informed everything she's done since.

FRAN DE'ATH

Fran became known as the woman who invited people for tea in her tipi, immortalised in the photograph by Edward Barber of her sitting in front of a large sign saying, 'Hello can you stop for a talk?'

FRANKIE ARMSTRONG

Frankie is a folk singer who has sung professionally in the women's and peace movements since the 1960s. She experienced Greenham as someone without sight, including dealings with police and their horses, and, of course, through the power of song.

GILLIAN BOOTH

Gillian was a Greenham stalwart whose accounts of living at Main/ Yellow Gate bring the camp vividly to life. She created one of the camp's favourite songs, known by many as 'Down at Greenham on a Spree', though she originally wrote it as 'Here at Greenham on a Spree'. Gillian was part of a group of women who took their political activism to America and illegally entered the Pentagon.

HANNAH SCHAFER

Hannah was a Blue Gate resident, where she participated with gusto in the female-centric camp life, telling her interviewer that 'if I had to pick one word to describe my life at Greenham it would have been fun with a capital F'. As her mother's family were Quakers and both her parents were involved in the Aldermaston marches in the 1950s, Hannah describes herself as having grown up 'with the peace movement as part of my life'.

HAZEL PEGG

Hazel was a resident of Main/Yellow Gate. She was active in the women's strategy to overwhelm the courts and prisons. Through their barrister Helena Kennedy, she once pleaded self-defence to her charge, 'because we were committing a crime to prevent a greater crime'. After being issued with a fine, Hazel refused to pay. This strategy helped to fill up the prisons, exposing the unjust and illogical approach of the judicial system to convict women for non-violently campaigning for peace.

HELEN MACRAE

Originally from London and now living in Cornwall, Helen co-founded a support group for Greenham called Camden Women Against Cruise after attending Embrace the Base.

ILLONA LINTHWAITE

Illona is an actor and director based in London. From an early age, she had strong feelings about the unfairness of class and gender roles in society, and has been involved in the peace movement all her life.

JADE BRITTON

Involved in various women's groups, including Women for Life on Earth, Jade first visited Greenham in the early 1980s, later deciding to live at Violet Gate permanently for two years.

JANE GRIFFITHS

Jane went to Main Gate while she was at school in York and moved to camp permanently for about a year after she left school. She was arrested many times and went to Holloway and Styal prison as well as to a young offenders' institution because she was so young.

JANET SMITH

Remarkably, Janet hand-wrote her entire PhD thesis at Greenham during a time when there were daily evictions. She remembers it being anarchic but not chaotic – a community of women who, in her words, 'had your back'.

JENNY ENGLEDOW

Jenny was a figure at Greenham throughout its existence, watching the camp change and develop until its closure, collecting banners, photographs and keeping a personal archive from the camp.

JILL 'RAY' RAYMOND

Ray spent most of her time at Greenham living at Blue Gate. She holds the Blue Gate diaries for Greenham women to read and for the benefit of future generations of protestors.

JOSETTA MALCOLM

Josetta lived at Blue Gate in the mid to late 1980s. They remember a time of wild parties, as well as the development of political consciousness, especially in relation to Black and intersectional feminism.

JUDE MUNDEN

Jude left home at the age of 15 and joined the Fallout Marching Band, an anti-nuclear street-protest band based in London. With them, she went to Greenham. Today she works as a theatre designer and maker in theatre, film, opera and exhibitions.

JUDITH BARON

Arriving at Greenham Common from the CND movement, Judith began visiting in around 1984/85. Taking a year off college, she spent a transformative nine months living at Greenham and went on to be a visitor at Aldermaston Women's Peace Camp for eleven years. A keen visual artist, Judith also produced a book of her photography from her time at Greenham.

JUDY HARRIS

Judy was 25 when she joined the Embrace the Base demonstration. She moved to Yellow Gate at the beginning of 1984. After a few months, she moved to Orange Gate.

KAREN FISHER

Karen first came to Greenham for the Embrace the Base action with friends in her twenties, and remained there for around eighteen months. She believes Greenham saved her life.

LORNA RICHARDSON

Lorna was involved in her local CND group from the age of 14, and learned about Greenham through the Quakers. She first hitched to Green Gate with two friends when she was 16 and stayed at Turquoise Gate. Lorna has travelled all over the world campaigning for peace, including protesting at a site in Nevada just before a British nuclear bomb was detonated by the US military.

LYN BARLOW

Lyn left care at 18 and took a student trip to Greenham, visiting regularly afterwards and moving there permanently three years later. Lyn's attitude to non-violence informed her engagement with MoD soldiers and squaddies. She believes Greenham can teach valuable lessons in critical thinking that are just as relevant to young women today.

LYNETTE EDWELL

Lynette was a local woman who opened her home to Greenham women and made many friendships which have continued. She was part of the Cruise Watch press team, collating reports of the convoy dispersals and sending them to national and international media. In addition, she took part in life at the camp, joining demonstrations and blockades, and campaigning against injustice to the women by the police, military and courts.

LYNNE WILKES

Lynne was on the Night Watch team, largely for Blue Gate. Today, she uses what she learned at Greenham about the way in which women supported one another to inform her practice working with vulnerable people.

MAGGIE O'CONNOR

Maggie O'Connor was most involved with Indigo and has carried away from that gate the sense of how important singing was at Greenham, allowing protestors to tackle fear by doing something about it in a creative and empowering way.

MAGGIE PARKS

Finding Greenham at the time of her father's death, Maggie allowed the energy and love at the camp to swell into the void and become a vital part of her understanding of grief and healing. The experience has stayed with her in a lifelong career supporting and protecting women against violence.

MARGARET MCNEILL

Margaret went to Greenham after getting involved in the local CND movement. She was profoundly influenced by the discussions at Greenham and left with a radical feminist perspective on the peace movement that changed the course of her life.

MARIA RAGUSA

Maria visited Greenham regularly and taught self-defence to the women, navigating the politics involved in mixing self-defence and NVDA.

MARIE KNOWLES

While secretary of Camberley CND and co-organiser of local feminist consciousness-raising groups, Marie was an avid supporter of Greenham, taking part in demos and actions, Night Watch and Cruise Watch. She took her first child, Rebecca, to Greenham when Rebecca was 5. With the support of her loving partner, John, Marie later moved to Cornwall with her family where she ran a health food shop, became financial director of a company and a Relate counsellor, all while home-schooling Rebecca and her younger brother Dickon.

MARY BIRCH

Mary and her husband played an active role at Greenham in the 1980s. They regularly drove from Bristol to Newbury in their van to transport goods to the women, such as firewood and blankets.

MICA MAY

Mica came to the peace movement accidentally while living in Manchester and visited Greenham for the Embrace the Base action. Describing it as a transformational experience, Mica lived at Yellow Gate in 1983. With her partner, Hattie, she now runs Stopcocks Women's Plumbers and they have established the country's first Register of Tradeswomen.

NINA MILLNS

Nina is a writer, actor and activist and attended a nursery established by Greenham women. Operating through a non-hierarchical and collective decision-making process they, some as openly gay and bisexual women, encouraged the children to explore their identities – something Nina believes was a direct result of their own Greenham experiences.

PEGGY SEEGER

Peggy is a folk singer, songwriter and activist who wrote the famous camp song 'Carry Greenham Home'. Along with other musicians, she sang to the marchers who were coming through from Wales to Greenham in 1981. She later joined them at Greenham.

PENNY GULLIVER

Penny was 21 when she took a break from writing and performing in theatre and went to Greenham. She stayed for a year at Blue Gate, experiencing one of the most severe eviction periods.

SALLY HAY

Sally's belief is that language is critical in making attitudinal changes. She describes the challenges to the standard discourse that Greenham women made as 'little prods on the wheel of a giant ship'. Gradually the ship turns and then it carries on turning and eventually a noticeable change of direction has taken place.

SARAH GREEN

Sarah is an environmental campaigner who is involved in the HS2 protests. She gave up her job to live at Greenham Common in 1981 and stayed at Yellow Gate for around five years, giving birth to her son at camp.

SUE BOLTON

Sue was a regular visitor to the camp, disseminating the women's strategies of NVDA in her area. She was part of a contingent of women chosen to go to the USA during the legal action against President Reagan; their group became known on their native Isle of Wight as the Ventnor Peace Women.

SUE SAY

Sue went to prison many times; she was part of a team that took the authorities to court for illegal strip-searches and won, resulting in a law change.

TAMSIN CLAYTON

Tamsin arrived at Greenham in 1983 with her 2-year-old daughter, and although she started at Blue Gate, she and others with children decided to re-establish Red Gate.

VICKI SMITH

Vicki initially went to Greenham as a weekend visitor and later lived at Blue Gate for about two years. She was a founding member of Cruise Watch, a group that aimed to monitor and disrupt military manoeuvres on Salisbury Plain (which meant she often got to watch herself on television!).

1

SHALL THERE BE WOMANLY TIMES?

Where it all began

KATE KERROW AND REBECCA MORDAN

Shall there be womanly times or shall we die?
Are there men unafraid of gentleness?
Can we have strength without aggression,
Without disgust,
Strength to bring feeling to the intellect?
Shall we change or shall we die?
There shall be womanly times, we shall not die.

From 'Womanly Times', by Frankie Armstrong

'We wanted it to be talked about everywhere (…) We wanted to convey the alarm we felt at this dangerous time (…) I remember us saying we wanted Greenham to become a household word.'

Ann Pettitt and Karmen Thomas

On 5 September 1981 a group of women arrived at RAF Greenham Common in Berkshire, exhausted but tenacious.[2] They had walked an epic 110 miles and now, inspired by their foremothers the Suffragettes, promptly began chaining themselves to the RAF base fence. They had named themselves Women for Life on Earth.

Little did these women realise how connected they were to those awesome first-wavers who inspired them in their chaining up; their march began an almost twenty-year campaign, becoming the largest women-only political demonstration since Suffrage. Between 1981 and 2000, thousands of women would come to Greenham to demand debate. They would make history, demonstrating the importance and effectiveness of peaceful protest and, in the process, they were to radicalise an entire generation.

In some senses, the women's march was intended as a media campaign, a response to the low-level press coverage of the missiles being held at Greenham; the holding of such weaponry was being presented to the public as normal and underwhelming – truly everything the missiles were not.

NATO, fearing the SS-20 Sabers which were introduced into the Soviet rocket forces in 1976 – terrifying inventions that were deliberately developed to be mobile and to be launched with virtually no notice – deployed similar missiles at locations across Europe to show retaliation was possible.[3] Ninety-six BGM-109G ground-launched missiles and Pershing II ballistic missiles were to be held at Greenham Common.[4] Some sources state that each Pershing II ballistic missile was up to 100 times as powerful as the atomic bomb dropped on Hiroshima.[5]

While Britain appeared in slumber, the women were awake. They wouldn't sit by and watch as the escalating nuclear arms race readied the world for full-scale nuclear war. While men were making all the decisions about nuclear warfare – political strategy, the weaponry, weapon deployment – women's voices were being suppressed and submerged.

The women hadn't felt the decision to make the march woman-led was radical, but they remembered people's resistance to the woman-led nature of the protest: *Bombs don't discriminate, why should we protest?* But the women felt strongly that they, the other half of the population, had no voice in decisions that had grave impacts upon their lives. As such, the pamphlet they created to advertise the march was designed to appeal to women and gather them together. On one side it showed a deformed baby, like the ones who were, almost forty years later, still being born in Japan after Hiroshima.

'Why are we walking 110 miles? And then you turn over [the pamphlet] and there's this child – this is why,' said Ann Pettitt, one of the co-founders of Women for Life on Earth. 'It's not just the blast [...] radiation goes on killing and affects the unborn and the youngest.'

'Can you imagine,' Ann asked, referencing the fact that the missiles held at Greenham sat under American jurisdiction, 'if this had still been around when we have a president like Trump?' At the time of writing, Donald Trump's presidency is over, but it is important to note that he withdrew America from the 1987 Intermediate-Range Nuclear Forces Treaty in 2019,[6] arousing concern at his interest in building once-banned nuclear missiles, very similar in their readiness and portability to those held at Greenham. In our conversations with the Greenham women, all consistently recalled the sense of urgency around the very real nuclear threat in the early 1980s, and their sense of terror at the reckless injustice and devaluing of human life. More than one woman, when talking of her fears, referenced the lyrics of a famed Greenham song, the crackling camp recording to which we listened to many times, inspired by the energised, liberated shout-sing calls of the women, wild, raucous and tribal:

What d'you need more atom bombs for?
You got enough bombs to kill us all ten times
Yet still you keep asking for more.
Take those toys away from the boys
Take those toys away from the boys.

It was 1980 when Ann began considering the idea of organising a protest march from Wales to the RAF base at the common. She tried hard to awaken interest in the idea but struggled to find any take-up. That is, until her partner, who attended their local CND meetings, came home one day and mentioned there was a woman in the group whom he felt might offer her support. He put the two women in touch and Ann was to meet Karmen Thomas, a young woman who was as horrified at the plans for Britain to host the missiles as she was.

Neither woman realised at the time, but this was the second time it had been suggested that they should meet. The pair first met in London in 1977, when Ann was pregnant and Karmen had just given birth to a little boy. On that first occasion it was their shared midwife who had felt there would be a connection between them. A pregnant Ann visited Karmen in her home just after she had given birth, and recalled the delicate fragility of the post-childbirth experience. They remembered very little else about the meeting, though both would call their sons Ben.

So Ann went to Karmen's house for what she thought was her first meeting with this inspiring potential colleague. Ann's partner had been right; Karmen's enthusiasm for the idea was immediate. With their collective energy, the pair quickly recruited two other women, and regular meetings began occurring at Karmen's house. But it was only after two or three visits that Ann said she started to feel a sense of familiarity. This sense of familiarity grew and eventually found its way into conversation. When the two women realised they had already met in London when they were both entering into motherhood, a sense of purpose emerged. Ann told us: 'We had to do it.'

The two women recalled their haste to organise the march, despite the fact that they had no money, were struggling at that time to pay domestic bills and had to rely on a small loan from the CND to get the protest up and running. *Cosmopolitan* magazine offered them a tiny free advert, and they set to letter writing and rallying contacts. But they were often questioned about the structure of their organisation. Karmen told us: 'You'd ring somebody up and they'd say "So who do you represent?" and we went "Well, who *do* we represent?"'

This was where the title Women for Life on Earth came from. She and Ann laughed: 'Talk about arrogance! But it wasn't an organisation, we were just women for life on earth. Simple.' Karmen explained that she spent a lot of time putting coins into phone boxes, calling newspapers and trying to get coverage, even going up to the press hub of London's Fleet Street the night before the march to get attention for the

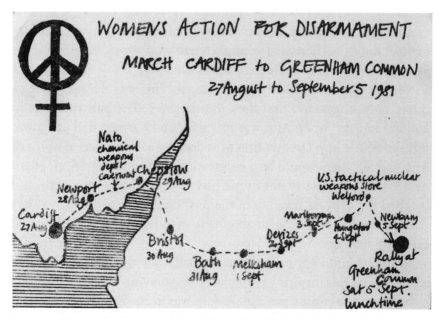

A map of the route the march took from Cardiff to Greenham. (Sue Lent)

story. 'They just didn't want to know,' she said. When asked why she felt there was so little up-take, she felt the attitude was: '"Peace? Boring. We did that last year."'

Around forty people responded to their call for marchers and very few were women they knew. 'We thought there's maybe just going to be a dozen people turn up,' Karmen said. But those forty who responded to the call mostly also arrived to march that day – Thursday, 27 August 1981. Karmen commented that, had she hand-picked the group, there couldn't have been a more varied crowd with their differing ages, professions and geographical homes.

Among them was a woman who would become one of the key figures in the Greenham Common Women's Peace Camp. Then 44 years of age, Helen John was working as a nurse and was very new to politics. On that 110-mile walk, Helen would use her medical skills to help the other women treat their tired feet, and they all received a foot inspection from her every day. She would go on to spend ten years living on the common, pioneering the strategies of NVDA, and being arrested thirty-two times for criminal damage alone. She would be one of the first people to be charged under new anti-terror legislation for walking 15ft across a sentry line at RAF Menwith Hill, which housed a US eavesdropping operation run by the US National Security Agency.[7]

There was also Sue Lent, who arrived with her husband and their baby 'in the pushchair [...] he was just turned a year [...] Fortunately, I was breastfeeding him, so I didn't have to worry too much about bottles and all the rest of it.'

The marchers had a police escort most of the way, and they swapped escorts at the county borders. Police tried to specify routes but the women held fast; they knew which way they wanted to go. Karmen felt there was a patronising concern for 'you ladies' being injured or harmed, but also fear at the idea of a woman causing confrontation in public.

Despite the support of Cardiff CND, Karmen said she felt a sudden and overwhelming responsibility for the marchers. As organisers, she and Ann were responsible for their welfare, for feeding them, for providing shelter, and although she enjoyed the march, she remembers it was challenging from a financial perspective. 'I mean, today you could just go and stick it on a credit card or whatever. There'd be that at the back of your head,' she said. Despite the pressure the organisers were under, in her interview, Sue praised them for the care and attention they'd shown: 'What a complete revelation it was [...] everywhere we stopped, it was so well organised, they'd got lunch everywhere – it was food, food, food [...] Good accommodation with families.'

Sue, Karmen and Ann all recalled it being very hot that August, and the main response wasn't one of support, but mostly of bewilderment as the women trudged across county borders, holding their children's hands, worn down by the burning heat. Sue remembered the police using the heat as a bargaining tool to get the women off the roads: 'We were continually being offered a lift in the police car, because of course we'd got the baby [...] all the way along really to Greenham, you know, they'd say "Do you want a lift? You've got the baby." And you'd think "No! I'm going to walk!", while absolutely pouring with sweat.'

Despite the efforts of the organisers and police fears of them causing a fuss in public, the women attracted little press attention. But the march *was* making an impact on its marchers. Sue talked warmly of the performances that had been arranged for them at each stop: Peggy Seeger and Ewan MacColl in Melksham, Dorothy Thompson and Frankie Armstrong in Bristol, and Bruce Kent and Pat Arrowsmith would be waiting to entertain the women when they finally arrived at the common. Additionally, Karmen remembered three male students had marched with the women from Cardiff to Newport, and instead of leaving when they'd planned, they decided they wanted to stay on. They committed to support roles such as looking after the children or organising practicalities, leaving their part-time jobs to walk alongside the women. 'If it hadn't been for one of them, we wouldn't have had a record of it, a photographic record, a visual record [...] we hadn't thought about taking cameras, there was all the other stuff going on,' Karmen said.

Women for Life On Earth soon bonded. Sue told us: 'We'd developed this jovial style, we'd all started singing and dancing.' They were also evolving into a tolerant, nurturing group. While saying that at that time she didn't consciously identify as a feminist, Ann credits the two self-identified feminists on the walk for this special group dynamic who, she said, had told of how they had communicated in their women's groups. They shared a method whereby everyone would say their feelings one by one and no one else was allowed to voice dissent or support – everyone was just to listen. 'They did suggest that,' Ann said. 'And it was absolutely invaluable.'

This group dynamic was essential for the next stage, where two of the women suggested more radical action to attract much-needed attention. The idea that they chain themselves to the base fence was raised and the group entered into discussion. 'That discussion was crucial,' said Ann. 'Whatever we did, we didn't want a small group of us to do it, and the rest to feel nervous or unhappy.' But many were opposed, believing that radical action of that type didn't echo their reasons for attending the march. One of the experienced activists in the group felt it would be divisive, and noted it could easily turn violent if the police responded aggressively.

Then a woman named Eunice spoke. Ann manifested Eunice's booming voice, the deep Welsh accent: '"What are we all so afraid of?" she'd said. "So what if a few helmets roll? What's worse than a nuclear war? I'll do it."' Eunice was an older, more experienced woman and carried a certain power. The women sat together and remembered the importance of what they were doing and why they had come. Ann felt Eunice's words served to suddenly disintegrate group opposition to the idea: 'Every person who spoke after that just said, "Fine".' Sue also remembered Eunice as inspirational – 'She was a Labour council-lor in Swansea [...] in her sixties [...] very feisty' – and recorded in her diary that when a male marcher spoke out against the women chaining themselves up, Eunice had told him: 'We've come all this way, we're not gonna go home for nothing [...] And you know, women have done things in the past a lot more dangerous. I'll chain myself up!'

The women arrived at the common at around 7 a.m., and several went straight to the fence to begin chaining themselves up. Karmen went to the policeman guarding the entrance, in her hand a declaration of the women's intentions, handwritten in the pub the night before.

'You're early,' the policeman said, before Karmen opened her mouth to speak. The warnings about the police being prepared for the women, and potentially having riot vans ready and waiting, flooded her mind. She laughed: 'I thought, Jesus, they knew we were coming!'

In fact, the policeman had merely mistaken her for the cleaner. Just as Karmen was about to boldly read the declaration, a car pulled up full of keening women, loudly heralding their support. Despite the strange scene, and then Karmen telling the guard there were women chained to the fence, he barely raised an eyebrow. 'He seemed to find it was normal! Maybe he'd read up on the Suffragettes and thought "This is what women do!"'

The women wanted the commander to come out of the base and talk with them, but he refused. Sue said that at this point 'some people started to disperse', but 'a lot of people stayed'. Ann said she herself stayed on for a week at the base, while the women took turns to be chained up. There was very little press interest, and the few reporters who did show up were mainly, depressingly, only interested in seeing a woman in chains. A few of the women went to a jumble sale in Newbury, made some dummies

Women regularly blockaded fence gates at Greenham and at other bases all over the country in order to restrict the manoeuvres of the military, such as vehicles coming in or out, by sitting down, linking arms and singing. (Sandie Hicks)

with stockings, and dressed them up in jumpers, scarves and hats, then chained them to the fence instead. When the reporters turned up asking for the women in chains, they would direct them to the dummies. Ann says of one such reporter: 'He came back and he said, "Okay, very funny", and I said, "Well, you want dummies in chains, so there you are," and he then said, "Fair enough. So why are you here?"'

Ann replied: 'Well, thank you for asking. You're the first one who's asked.'

News spread of the women's walk and supporters began travelling to the base, equally as convinced as the marchers that the global arms race could lead to nuclear war. Many had already been at other peace camps, such as nearby Aldermaston or Faslane in Scotland.

According to most accounts, meetings to discuss whether the camp should be women-only happened within the first few weeks of the marchers setting up at Greenham. However, the discussion appears to have taken place repeatedly, with many different attendees, though most believe the camp finally ended up as officially women-only by February 1982. This was some four months after Women for Life on Earth first arrived at the common. However, while the women's opinions differ about at what point the camp became meaningfully man-free, all the accounts state that male visitors were allowed in the day. Several women brought up male children at the camp, and Green Gate was the only space that was women-only twenty-four hours a day, seven days a week.

But why was Greenham women-only?

Many women felt, based on past experience as campaigners or just on their lived experience, that men dominated space verbally and physically, and little room was left for women to communicate and participate equally, let alone make decisions or drive action.

Sue Say, who would go on to live at the camp for over two years, described how in 1981 she was working as a trainer for a Swedish company:

> We were going into businesses and telling them how to work better to achieve more profit. During the process of working for Halfords, I looked at it and I could see very clearly what the problem was: men did not trust what women said. And so our advice to that company had to be to take the women off the counters, and shove them into the back rooms in the offices, and I think it broke me. I think that just made me feel so sick inside. Business-wise, it was practical, logical, sensible, but in my head, I thought, 'I can't do this. I can't keep being part of oppressing women'.

Later, women also observed that the men at the camp, though political allies, failed to participate in the everyday chores. 'They didn't do the washing up, help with the food, look after the kids,' explained Jill 'Ray' Raymond, known as X-Ray at her Blue Gate home. 'This was really early days and so it was quite tied up with "If we're going to stay here, and we want to be non-violent, how can we do it? We can't do it with the men around because they get drunk, they are violent and they won't do the washing up. They expect us to cook for them."' Numerous women described to us how they felt that men only saw the excitement, the cause, but not all the underpinnings that make a camp work; nor did they see it was largely women who were labouring away at all that work in the background. This desire to deconstruct and challenge the gendered roles of women and men would recur throughout Greenham's existence, informing the way the women organised the camp, used language and planned actions.

We also heard repeatedly from women that there was concern that it would be harder, if not impossible, to operate the policy of NVDA if men stayed at the camp and took active roles in camp-based actions. Women described feeling that men were reticent about enacting the requirements of passive resistance – to relax the body and be carried away by the police – and instead found themselves in arguments that escalated tensions.

Sally Hay, whose first visit to the camp was in 1980, agreed. She arrived with her then partner:

One particular Sunday [...] before it became a women's camp [...] I remember we were at what became known as Main Gate, and there was a sort of rush – because the police were very violent in the way they pushed people back. And I was horrified. And we were both shocked by it. But my partner became – I felt – quite excited by the aggression [...] Later, we stayed on talking to people, and everybody was doing as people do following a large emotional event – going through their individual perspectives of what they saw, what they heard, and how dreadful it was. And I became aware there was a meeting going on, at which women older than me, more vocal, and a great deal more competent, were saying, 'This is the problem of having men at the camp' [...] and I remember quietly thinking to myself, 'Wow' [...] I know it sounds silly, but this chimed with what I was feeling about what I'd seen and heard – that it was the men. Both male police officers, but also the male protestors – it was men.

Overall, the women who pushed for Greenham to be a women-only camp did so because they felt this was the best way for women to take up their own space and ensure the direction of the camp; rather than excluding men, the aim was to include women.

But there were others who felt very differently. Ray – who had come to Greenham to vote for the camp to be women-only – acknowledges that this decision cut both ways: 'Some heterosexual women left Greenham at that point, because they said, "The lesbians can live here with their lovers but we can't, so we're not going to stay."' Betty Levene, already a seasoned peace campaigner when she arrived at Greenham, says she soon left after the early meetings discussing making the camp women-only. 'It was just targeting the wrong men,' she sighed. 'These gentle guys I was with weren't the problem, it just felt wrong to me that they were unwelcome.'

In 1981, the same year that Ann, Karmen and Women for Life on Earth marched to Greenham, Becky Griffiths started sixth form in Kendal. She also joined the local CND.

At first she wasn't a particularly passionate member, going along to meetings because 'it just felt right', but all this was to change when her group responded to Greenham's call to Embrace the Base.

Embrace the Base, which took place in December 1982, was the first major national action of the camp's life and widely exceeded the activists' hopes of attendance and scale. Women and girls came from all across the UK and beyond to hold hands around the 9-mile perimeter of the RAF military enclosure in what would be one of the largest women-only demonstrations in history.

The experience changed Becky forever. 'It was amazing,' she told us. 'I don't remember the journey there or back, but I remember getting to the main gate and seeing this amazing-looking woman with a walkie-talkie just organising stuff. I was blown away by it.' Still a schoolgirl, Becky described her awe at seeing 'hundreds of women there, surrounding the base, incredible and powerful. I felt really thrilled by it.' Explaining the conviction the camp inspired in her, she thought: 'I've got to come back. I've got to come back and be here.'

She went home and told her mother her feelings. When asked about her A levels, Becky pointed out: 'Yeah, well, the world's going to blow up. There's no point in doing A-Levels, you know, I've got to save the world.'

In invoking her younger self, Becky smiled: 'I was quite literal and slightly teenage about it all.' But at the same time, she remembered a sense of knowing that Greenham was absolutely where she should be. In the end, her mother agreed: 'I think I spent Christmas at home, and then she drove me down from Cumbria, and we sort of made a tent out of plastic, and that was it.' So Becky moved to Greenham; her mother joined her in early 1983. Both were to live at Main Gate/Yellow Gate for the next two years. As the camp developed, the women would have a choice about where they lived on the site. They created 'gates', each one known by a different name, each one developing its own character and value system and resultant way of working.

Commenting on how things ran day to day, Becky reflected:

> I suspect as is with any world, people sort of fell into things that they liked doing. Some people were great at cooking, and some people were great at keeping the fire going, so there didn't feel like there was any tension around that. Possibly it might have gone over my head, but my memory of it is that I can't remember any conflict about the day-to-day running of it, and it seemed to work.

This was interestingly opposite to her memory of spending some time with the American Peace Corps a few years later. 'They were definitely more organised,' she said. 'There were lots of rotas for this, that and the other – but we were quite frustrated by the extent of the talking, and desperate to just go and do stuff.'

Talking was a dominant feature at Greenham too, however. Determined not to mirror the patriarchal structures they had seen around them, the women were committed to the principle of non-hierarchical organisation. There were no appointed leaders and time was made for everyone to have their say – which meant many, often rather long, meetings. 'We tried to make decisions by consensus,' Becky explained. 'So there was a camp meeting, and decisions were made about actions. Decisions were made about money, because we received loads of donations of money coming into the camp, and there were decisions made about what to do with that – if we were spending it, did we all agree with that decision?'

The camp appeared to run along the anarchist principle that each woman was her own leader, taking responsibility for her own actions and their effect on others and the community as a whole. However, when the wider world impacted upon the camp, in the form of issues related to money, court cases and the media, for example, meetings were held 'and obviously, people didn't always agree with each other – people might not have agreed with actions – but as long as they were within the non-violent code, then what one person chose to do was fine, even if someone else wouldn't have chosen to do it'.

Once the camp was established, the women lived outside all year round. The number of women living or visiting at any one time varied, but there were some who lived outside without electricity or mains water in any and all weathers, several telling us about how they would wake up under frozen blankets that could be snapped in two. 'You had to wear a lot of clothing. The life of the camp was around the fire, for obvious reasons,' Becky recalled. 'It was miserable if it rained and everything was muddy. There were times when it was extremely cold.'

At first, the women lived in tents but the local council soon employed bailiffs to evict them. In response, the women created a more light-weight and portable shelter which they called a 'bender': a structure made of cloth, or plastic sheets, thrown over a sapling that was bent over and tethered to the ground – an adaptation of a traditional technique used by their nomadic, prehistoric foremothers, who had used hide for the purpose. 'Those benders, you can get them quite warm if you light lots of candles,' Becky told us.

She described how there were two or three local people at the Newbury Quaker Meeting House who would let the women use their hot water and washing machines, but support was by no means unanimous:

A lot of it was quite contentious. There was a lot of difficult press about 'filthy lesbians', and we were living outside – you look very

The Greenham women often hand drew and designed leaflets, flyers and newsletters for their events. (LSE Women's Library)

different from the rest of the world when you're living outside – and Newbury is not an alternative town. It's a small conservative English town and we were not small conservative women. Occasionally people would shout from cars as they went by. There was an antagonistic attitude. We were not of their world.

Still, undeterred by the judgement of locals and the press, the women created their own world at camp; a world where they experimented with emotions, with art, humour and education. 'We tried to do things that were funny and creative and playful,' Becky explained:

> We made amazing banners all the time. And those were constantly evolving and changing, and people sang all the time. And those songs were constantly evolving and changing. And you know, nobody had mobile phones, or tablets, or any of that. So we made our own world really, and I think that's part of it, the conversation and creativity, the sparking off each other. That's definitely a whole world, a full world is, isn't it?

We asked every woman we interviewed what one memory or feeling arose when they thought of Greenham. 'Woodsmoke' was a frequent answer, reflecting the women's sensory memories of camp. But to this question, Becky replied: 'Freedom, I think.'

2

WE'LL STAY HERE AT GREENHAM

Daily life at camp

REBECCA MORDAN

They say they're protecting the women and kids
But they're building their bunkers just for government 'Bigs'
These bombs make us victims, it's us who will die
We'll stay here at Greenham, we'll stay here at Greenham
We won't move from Greenham, ain't trusting their lies.

'Silos Song', by Rebecca Johnson

'Sitting around the fire with a group of women that you'd never really met before (…) who might be from, I don't know London, Holland, or Alaska. And you just have a conversation. And it usually starts with "Where have you come from?" And the next question was sometimes "How long have you been here?" And that could be twenty minutes or four years. I always used to carry a pen knife with me, and I would just always be whittling tent pegs, before another muncher would come and take the tents away (…) I play the recorder and I met a woman who also played the recorder, and neither of us knew the same tunes or music, but we played our recorders together and it worked.'

Alison Napier

A woman arriving at camp for the first time might be subject to a wide variety of first impressions. It might be a winter Saturday morning, with thousands of women pouring off buses, climbing out of cars, walking up from the station, singing. There might be women crowding around the 10ft military fence topped with razor wire, preparing to rock it or cut it down en masse. The ground might be very muddy, the raised voices and cloudy breath of hundreds of women filling the air and the smell of woodsmoke pervading everything.

Or maybe it's a Monday evening in summer, the weekenders and visitors have gone and the remaining women sit in small groups around campfires preparing cups of tea or food. They chat about setting off for the long walk to Yellow Gate to get water, or they drift off in ones and twos to collect yet more firewood. The ground might be a little less muddy. Here and there a woman's voice carries across the air in song, laughter or shout, and pervading everything is the smell of woodsmoke.

What part of the camp you arrived at, or lived at, what time of year you were there and for how long, and what event you might have come for were all factors that changed the character of the camp and these account for the diverse variety of memories and impressions the women gave us of it.

Striking to any new arrival, and certainly not lost on the Greenham women, was the stark visual contrast between nature and 'man'. On one side of the camp were the rolling green spaces and ancient woodlands of one of Britain's last and largest areas of common land (it is understandable that author Richard Adams, when living on the edge of Greenham, had chosen the common for the setting of *Watership Down*). On the other side, what had started as a perfunctory fence had grown to be a three-layer-deep, 9-mile fortification guarded by dogs and soldiers of the Ministry of Defence (MoD). Beyond this, the grey metal bunkers, massive air hangars, ominous watch towers, sprawling runways and identical concrete-box dwellings that housed the US personnel and their families. UK squaddies lived within the fence too, put up in military tents in all weathers; their dwellings were a far cry even from the basic homes provided for their American counterparts – as some Greenham women pointed out to soldiers through the fence.

Some of the gates were in more wooded parts of the common, such as Green and Emerald, giving them a different atmosphere to gates closer to the military fence, like Yellow. (Sandie Hicks)

Depending which road she had come in on, or the bent of her temperament, a woman might drift into conversation at the camp she was nearest to, settling there, at least for now, in a spirit of easy sisterhood. Or she might decide to wander the perimeter of the RAF base. At every military gate, different camps named after colours of the rainbow had sprung up, each with a different character. The new arrival might stay and hope to find her kind at one, share her time between several, or even set up a new one of her own.

Dr Janet Smith told us:

The Main Gate became a lot of Black women, the Green Gate became kind of all goddess-y. And the Blue Gate was very much northern working class, and it was kind of interesting [...] it wasn't fragmentation, it was diversification really. And that was the strength of having small groups who kind of networked with each other as a structure, rather than having someone going, 'Today we're going to do this, and this is how it will work. And you'll do that'. It just wouldn't have survived like that, I don't think.

The first and largest gate at Greenham was originally called Main Gate. It was located outside the main gates of the base, where Women for Life on Earth had originally arrived. As other gates were set up, a collective decision was made to refer to them by colours to avoid enacting hierarchies of language that the women felt propped up the patriarchy; just because the original camp had the most women at it didn't mean it should be seen as more important, or as the Main. To embrace this lateral language, Main Gate became Yellow Gate to most, though many early residents referred to it as Main for its duration.

'I would say Yellow Gate was my patch, or Main Gate as we used to call it,' explains Sue Say, who arrived at Greenham to live when she was just 18. 'I loved the Clearing,' she added, referencing the leafy offshoot to the side of Yellow Gate inhabited by mostly younger women:

> I would say each gate and area had a kind of feel to it. Most people would start off at Yellow Gate/Main Gate, and they would end up at the gate that was more appropriate. I would say I spent very little time at any other gate other than Yellow Gate, maybe Orange and Blue. Orange because that was where there were children and Blue because that was closest to the pub, is the truth. I went to Green Gate – that was way too cosmic for me!

Carolyn Francis had just come back from Canada, after dropping out of college in Bangor, Wales. The 'cosmic' nature of Green Gate was a positive draw for her in the summer of 1984, when she arrived. However, she described: 'My sister was Yellow Gate hardcore: snip through the fence, jump on the commander's bonnet, get locked up for a week in Holloway! She just really went for it!' This perception of the political, action-based, sometimes uncompromising nature of Yellow Gate was reinforced by the regular presence of the press, as well as it being the gate visitors often used to enter for large-scale actions, and where supporters left donations.

49

Despite being a crucial underpinning to the daily running of the camp, donations were not always without controversy. Hazel Pegg and Gillian Booth, who lived at Yellow Gate, recalled the divisive delivery of a Harrods hamper, which arrived complete with chauffeur, who picked his way through the mud to bring it to them. Though unable to agree on whether it was from Yoko Ono ('that nice woman!') or Linda McCartney ('there was a ham – Linda McCartney wouldn't have sent us that'), the two friends agreed that they had to step in when 'Katrina [...] wanted to throw the alcohol away'. Hazel explained: 'I just objected to throwing away Harrods champagne and wine – not often I'd seen that in my scene. And Katrina wanted to throw half of it away and I was just so upset. Well, I took direct action [...] I remember saying, "Just go back to your bender, Katrina. If you don't want it, the rest of us do!"'

Benders were just one of the ingenious ways in which the women created shelters at camp. Jane Griffiths described the versatility of benders:

Bits of tarpaulin, bits of plastic, bits of string – if we weren't being evicted, if we had sort of the possibility for more stable structures, then benders were amazing! You need quite a lot of bendy sticks. So you have some bendy sticks going vertically that combine at the top, and you tie them together. And then you have some bendy sticks going horizontally which weave in and out, and you tie them together until it's fairly stable, and at whatever size or shape you wish. I took my cello briefly and I had one that was tall enough for me to sit in it and play cello at one point.

Jane's friend Judy Harris elaborated on the varied capabilities of benders:

Annie had made this bender that was a kind of a collapsible bender that you could pick up and walk away with. And then Liz at Indigo made this bender on wheels, because she was American and she'd heard about how you could claim sanctuary in a church – her idea was, when they came to evict, she would push the bender down the road to the church that was near to Blue Gate and claim sanctuary there [...] And Sarah was pregnant, and she really wanted to have the baby at camp – that was really important to her [...] and the midwives

Rudimentary tents and 'benders' like these were where the majority of Greenham women slept. (Paula Allen)

were great about it actually because they were like, 'Oh yes, I think we can manage in here you know, we just need to make sure that it's hygienic' – in this bender like the size of a peanut!

Sure enough, Sarah Green had her baby in a bender at Yellow Gate – the only birth in the camp's history.

Across her four-year residency, Lorna Richardson recalled 'many a happy night in a "getaway"'. In response to the evictions and need for quick getaways from the rubbish truck nicknamed 'the muncher' by the women as it devoured their possessions, a Quaker:

invented this wonderful, wonderful tent – it was a single-skinned, single-person tent made out of three hoops, sort of a triangular tent [...] And you could literally un-pitch it [...] when you had to run by scooping your hands through the three hoops and picking the whole damn thing up off the ground [...] And somebody thought of and designed that and invented it and then raised up enough money from other Quakers, had a bunch of them made and then sent them to us. And they were brilliant!

Just as location and logic had dictated where the first of the Greenham camps formed, so Green Gate was set up in response to the silos being built to house the incoming cruise missiles. Jill 'Ray' Raymond remembered:

So Yellow Gate was on a lorry road down to Southampton, Blue Gate was a more sort of B-road, but the thing is at first there was only Yellow Gate – Main Gate – and then we gradually would open other gates temporarily for big actions, like Orange Gate and Blue Gate and Green Gate. Because Green Gate was right opposite the silos, we watched the silos being built, and a lot of vehicles were coming in and out of there – delivering the stuff to build the silos.

Despite its origin as a vantage point to keep an eye on the military developments, Green Gate soon got a reputation, as Maggie Parks told us, for being 'the spiritual gate', not least because 'it was right in the middle of the woods, and it became a bit witchy'. Maggie had come to Greenham at 30 after growing up in Jarrow ('my grandfather was on the Jarrow hunger march') and Malvern ('I ended up being a working-class kid on a council estate going to a very posh grammar school') and experimenting with the hippy movement and women's consciousness-raising groups. She recalls fondly how an average day might start at Green Gate: 'Oh, getting up late [...] 9 or 10 o'clock [...] Having cups of tea, sitting around. Visitors coming, talking to visitors, going off "wooding" – that's going off into the woods to get lots of fuel for the fire – going and getting water. Sometimes going to the shop, sometimes going into the swimming pool to take a shower.'

Judith Baron, whose stays at the camp included living at Green, Blue and Woad gates, described a similar impression of daily life:

You'd get up, and sometimes someone else had done the fire but if they hadn't you'd make the fire, and the day involved lots of tea – we were always making mugs of tea. And I just still have this vision of mud-crusted mugs! Especially in the winter when it's muddy. And toast. And that's when I got into marmite with tahini. Oh, nice! And also um, what was it? Garlic pickle. Sometimes would have that on toast.

[...] Often women would just turn up – you never knew who was going to turn up. You'd go out 'wooding' [...] Going to collect wood for the fire [...] there was a cricket bat factory not far away, but you needed someone with the car [...] and they didn't mind you having the off cuts, which was like really good, dry wood. It burned really quickly. So that was often good for starting the fire off, and then you'd go out and get logs or you might, if you'd found a big tree that was standing, you know, chop it up. And it was just sort of day-to-day things like that – going for a walk around the base.

Going in the base! [...] sometimes having meetings [...] a lot of it was sort of talking and tea and toast and cooking. In the evening, we'd have a communal meal – that was the only time we'd have a communal meal. It was usually some sort of vegetable stew, you know. In the winter, often there'd be a food round. So different local groups would have a different day, and they'd come round with food for everyone. Because sometimes – especially if it was wet and rainy, it would be really difficult to cook, because you couldn't get get the fire going [...] And there's a woman called Juliet who's still involved in Aldermaston – her food was really yummy! That day we'd get really excited, but it was appreciated just anyone bringing some food around [...] You might go into town [...] everyone used to put two pounds a day into a kitty [...] toast and vegetables for the main meal and that would come out of the kitty. So a lot of it was just day-to-day things, or talking to people [...] or going for a walk somewhere because the woods there were lovely.

Some of Carolyn Francis's most vivid memories bring to life the quirky and inventive nature of the eco-loving women at Green: 'I remember living inside this holly tree, someone had built a house right inside this holly bush, I used to sleep in there. And I really liked the bathroom tree – I thought it was such a great idea. It had mirrors hanging on it and then bowls of water around it [...] I've never forgotten that tree!'

Maggie also recalled the large international community of women from all around the world who were attracted to Green Gate:

It was just this amazing thing where women from all over came together [...] I made friends with a woman called Zol dé Ishtar, who was doing work about the nuclear bombing in the South Pacific and what was happening to people over there. So it became an international movement. And we were starting to make connections with women all over the world, and women were coming from America, Europe and Australia.

With regular visits from leading eco-feminists like Zol dé Ishtar, Monica Sjoo and Starhawk, Green Gate was soon a hub of goddess worship and alternative therapies. If women required healing or respite from camp pressures, they were likely to drop in at Green. This, and its policy of being completely women-only, without even allowing male visitors during the day, earned it the nickname of 'the Sanctuary'. It was also often the scene of conflict-resolution meetings when disputes occurred at other gates or between women.

Once the cruise missiles arrived at the base, another gate soon grew, around the military gates that were used to bring the convoys bearing the warheads in and out of the base from the local B-roads. This was Blue Gate, where, as Janet Smith explained, 'a lot of things happened all the time, it was quite full on [...] because they've got cruise missiles coming through, and if you happened to be there, and they're bringing cruise missiles in, you just have to go and lie in front of the gate'.

Penny Gulliver, arriving in October 1983, told us:

Basically we went down for three nights, and it was really cold, but on the third night I warmed up and went 'yeah, I can do this'. So we went back to London, packed a proper bag and we went back the following day, and I lived there for a year [...] Blue Gate chose us!

[...] It was dark when we got there – we got off the bus, we walked up the hill, because it was October and it wasn't late, but we'd gone and it was completely dark, and we didn't really know where we were going. We walked up the hill, and we could see something, which of course was a fire, and Blue Gate was the first gate that you come to if you walk out the town of Newbury, and so we stopped there. At that time it was called the Inter City Punk Gate, and it was, and the woman

I went with was from Bradford, and everybody was really from the north of the country, or they were Irish, Scottish or Welsh. And there was one other Southerner there at the time, and then there was two of us, really. And it was very working class, and very quickly you kind of understood – I think at that point there was four gates, or maybe – yeah it was probably only four – Yellow, Green, Orange and Blue. And then because over that winter and the spring, you know all the others popped up – Red, Turquoise [...] Yeah, so we stayed [...] it was a good fit, but it was an accident.

Remembering how the gates developed, she added: 'Turquoise set up just along from us, which was basically a vegan gate. Because most gates were vegetarian, everybody was vegetarian – even if you were a meat-eater, and there were meat-eaters at our gate, but they went into town and had chicken sandwiches and stuff, but Turquoise was a vegan gate.'

A few women at camp were decidedly not vegan, or even vegetarian, though they found themselves roundly outnumbered. Hannah Schafer, who came to Blue Gate from Liverpool after leaving school in 1983, recalled: 'One Christmas morning somebody bought us a Co-op turkey, and I was lying in bed and I heard them sending the turkey to the local old people's home and I was trying to shout while I was trying to put me clothes on: "No! Bring it back!"' By the time she had emerged from her tent, it was long gone.

Just as Turquoise had splintered from Blue to be vegan-only, so for a while Violet Gate was home to women who caved to being carnivores. Maria Ragusa, who had joined friends from CND at Violet, explained a joke before her interview that she and one of them used to share, telling us, 'All the other gates were very right-on [...] so me and Jade used to joke we were the right-off gate!'

Maria's friend and fellow Violet-Gater Jade Britton explained:

Violet Gate, it was known as the Violet Gate Slope, so you slid your way down it sometimes [...] you would be sitting there, around the fire-pit, and you could duck across the road and [...] there was a little path that led up to a little bit of clearing with trees and bushes, and on the other side of that was the golf course, so it was a nice stretch

The women came up with lots of ingenious strategies to help them deal with the evictions! (Dawn Stewart)

of green where you could build benders and things like that [...] there were gates there, but they never opened them, so you could park your vehicles up quite easily.

Her interviewer asked if there was any interaction with the golfers and Jade smilingly replied: 'Um, I think they were just kind of like disdainful, tried to ignore it and pretend it wasn't happening!'

Penny was living at 'Bloo', as it was called by many of its residents, when the council made a determined effort to evict the Greenham women using crews of bailiffs and a muncher that was fed with the women's tents and belongings sometimes several times a day: 'In the March of that year [1984] was when they started to come and clear the camps every day and so you were literally building a bender every day to sleep in, unless it was warm enough to sleep out. I got quite good at it [...] They'd take everything – all your benders, all your possessions: your boots, your sleeping bags, everything. If you weren't quick enough – the food, your pans, everything.' Ray agreed, remembering how the constant visits from the bailiffs at the height of the council's eviction campaign meant 'sleeping with your boots on'.

Fenja Hill described that at Red Gate they had 'this pram, that was our kitchen at Red Gate, and all our food [...] went in that, and then when they came around to evict us, we put everything in it and wheeled it away'.

Ray lived at Blue on and off for most of its duration and managed to help protect the camp's communal diaries from the bailiff's destruction time after time. 'Bloo Gate was very much on the frontline, you were right on the roadside, on the junction, and by the racecourse – near Newbury racecourse – so there was a lot of traffic, and it was the first stop coming up out of Newbury.' This meant that Blue Gate would usually be first on the bailiff's rounds, leaving the women living there little time to grab any belongings they didn't want to be thrown into the back of the muncher, though they would find time to dash ahead to other gates and issue warnings there. Ray recalled, laughing: 'The only good thing about the bailiffs is that they'd take the rubbish away!'

This sense of unconquerable irreverence explains Blue's reputation as the 'party' gate. While living mostly at Red Gate with her family, Tamsin Clayton admitted: 'I must say I did hang out quite a lot at Blue Gate, and I loved the Rokeby, which was the pub.' Women often stayed over at Blue on their way back from the Rokeby Arms, the only local pub that would, intermittently, serve Greenham women. The others in Newbury sported signs that frequently said things along the lines of: 'No dogs, Irish, Lesbians or Greenham Women'. Annie Brotherton, who arrived at Blue with Penny having gone to drama college with her, confirms: 'Yeah, Blue Gate was the northern gate, the one nearest the pub, Blue Gate was the rowdy gate!' But, as she points out, this proximity to the pub, and to drunken and hostile locals, also meant that:

Blue Gate was the one that got most of the hassle [...] it had a huge big teepee, when we first got there, and we all slept in the teepee. And then one, one night one of the neighbours came with a big Roses tin, you know, full of maggots and threw it in [...] then they set it on fire eventually one night, and people were in it. And so some of us had to stay up all night after that to keep the place safe.

Space and proximity from the road often played a part in the atmosphere of the Greenham gates. Just as Green enjoyed relative refuge by being in the woods, so Orange Gate benefitted from having space around it away from the road. Tucked round the corner from Yellow, Orange often held the creche on demo days. Margaret McNeill, a regular at such events through her local CND with her friends Annei Soanes and Marie Knowles, described how the creche 'was a good example of the men doing the women's work while the women got on with the demon-strating'. Marie's husband John was often one such man who recalled how, while his wife might be sitting in front of Margaret Thatcher's car or getting arrested for blockading with Annei and Margaret, he would be ensconced in the creche, making endless rounds of marmite sandwiches to feed the busloads of female campaigners – John warmly asserted: 'I was always a very willing accomplice!' Sadly, not all husbands were so accommodating, and one of the most frequent comments from interviewees about the husbands was the one that Margaret made to us: 'Of course, I'm not with him now.' Women often found that even men who supported the camp in theory struggled to maintain their support in practice. Sally Hay explained that her ex-husband 'nominally completely supported it, but I know that he was knocked [...] that men had been excluded [...] And that I was doing something independently of him, because he was a politico'. She went on to describe:

And I remember one particular occasion when we were having a meeting [...] about a mile or two's walk from where we lived, and I had left him with Emily – who was a breastfed baby. I had left two bottles of expressed milk and a bottle of sterilised water, in case of her waking up, and I was only out for about two hours anyway. But I remem-ber him walking around [...] with Emily wrapped in a vast quantity of woollen fabric, and thunderously hammering on the door and saying, 'You have abandoned your baby.' I said, 'Well didn't you give her the bottle?' And I remember him saying, and she would have been like six months old, 'She glared at me, and tried to punch me.' Oh for fuck's sake, she's a baby!

And he was terribly supportive notionally. As with, in fact, my flipping studies at the Bar [...] and he would always say he would babysit – and it knocks me when men call being at home alone with their babies 'babysitting' because it's ridiculous – and then would fail to turn up. Would fail to turn up home from work, and let me down [...] And I was constantly having to cancel grading meetings, because he would subvert [...] And in fact, I think the reality is that [...] Greenham was one of the factors of me becoming less of a nice girl, becoming more an independent woman, and someone with my own views, and someone who would do things independently of him. And ultimately, that didn't work [...] I left him in 1988.'

With this in mind, the presence of families at Yellow, Red, Indigo and Green and spaces like the creche at Orange became in and of themselves part of the radical politics of the camp, while showing how this radical feminism was nurturing, progressive and mature. Hazel Pegg, a long-term resident of Yellow Gate, recalled the 'quiet energy' of Orange 'because of the Quakers and the older women living up there'. Penny agreed: 'Yes, Orange Gate was definitely older at that time', adding, 'or it felt older to us – they were probably in their thirties! But there were lots of women there who'd been part of the Aldermaston marches and stuff, and it was lovely. They had settees at Orange Gate! They always had better cake! I don't know how they did it, but they did.'

Jade Britton felt that 'Orange Gate was the creative gate [...] people used to play musical instruments, and people would gravitate there, it was sort of arty [...] and they used to sometimes drive round in a van, and all of a sudden they'd leap out and perform some kind of skit or songs or something to entertain you, and then they'd all pile back in and drive off, so they were the entertainment gate.'

Parties and creativity were certainly not limited to Blue and Orange, however. Maggie remembered at Green that:

At night people would come and drum around the fire, and we'd sing, and we'd dance, and we'd read books and someone might read poetry to another, it was just amazing. I'd never lived out in nature before. I think the spiritual awareness [...] your real interconnectedness with nature, you know, literally living collectively together on the land. And of course, our periods started to sync and we got into moon magic and all of that stuff. So we celebrated the moons and, you know, did body painting. I mean, just crazy. You know, it was a really creative and intellectual ferment, it was just incredible.

On a day of festivities at Indigo, Maggie O'Conner remembers them putting on a puppet show; once it had played to its Greenham women audience, 'they turned all the screens around and showed it to the soldiers on the other side of the fence'.

Women also talked to us about the fluidity of occupying the camp; it wasn't just the women who moved around, but the locations of the camps themselves were sometimes subject to change. Ray explained the often lengthy process of finding a place to settle and how numerous the obstacles to setting up camp could be:

> I wasn't always at Blue Gate, you see we had to keep moving at Blue Gate, because they fenced a load of it off and said they were going to do a nature conservation area, and they fenced it off with this little picket fence and planted trees, so we had to move out. So we went on the other side of the road, and it got that you couldn't really put benders in the wood because of the evictions and the 'viggies' [vigilantes], so then we had [...] an old house, it was derelict I think, but the railings had hooks on, and we'd just have a huge long sheet of plastic and we all slept under there together ready for the, you know, 8 o'clock evictions.
>
> And then the Mormons got planning permission and built a Mormon church there, so the railings went [...] so then we moved to the other side of the road – the B-road – on a bit of green land that I don't think was part of the Common, because there was endless amounts of looking at maps and planning, and what was military and what was common [...] So then we had to move across [...] And they painted yellow lines, so then we couldn't park vehicles. So then I couldn't put my truck there any more, and back then I had a lover who also had a truck, so there was more room for both of us to be at Orange Gate.

Judy decided to move from Yellow to quieter Orange as a 'holiday' due to the number of visitors. 'There's a song that says, "Where do you get your water from?" and that is one of the questions that you just did get a lot,' she told us, laughing, referring to the popular camp re-working of 'In an English Country Garden' that included this verse:

What are all the questions the visitors will ask
at the Peace Camp, Newbury, Berkshire
I'll tell you some of those I know
and those I miss you'll surely ask –
How many of you are there here?
Is it cold and are you queer?
Where do you get your water from?
Do you shit in the gorse, will you die for your cause
at the Peace Camp, Newbury, Berkshire[8]

'And it's really important,' Judy continued, 'when you're in a group to be open to people coming in and everything, but it's actually very, very hard to sustain that, when people are coming all the time and asking exactly the same questions [...] Then there used to be this nightingale at Yellow Gate, and I can remember thinking, fucking nightingale, I wish it would shut up. So yeah, Orange – I really liked living there, and there was quite a lot of space to put benders and things up.' But after a while, Judy was motivated to move again. Fortified by her restorative time at Orange, she lived at the more visible gates again. 'It felt like we weren't really in the place we needed to be,' she said:

Because it was along that back road that they were bringing stuff out all the time. So then we moved round to Violet. And then we moved to Indigo, and I stayed at Indigo until I left. And that was quite tough, Indigo, because basically there was the verge and that was it. On the other side of the road was the golf club. And I remember one morning I was outside in front of Indigo Gate doing Tai Chi, and this golf club guy drove past in his Mercedes and went, 'Complete bloody nutter!', and wound his window up!

To add to the mercurial elements of camp life, the women regularly created other names for gates and areas, ranging from the signs of the zodiac to rune stones and gems. 'There ended up kind of nine or

Maggie Cook, a friend of the photographer's, demonstrating where and how the women went to the toilet at the camp – apparently the question most frequently asked by visitors after 'How do you get your water?' (Gini Mags)

so gates in that year,' Penny recalled about the end of 1983. 'I think Greenham was so big,' Alison Napier reflected. 'It was big enough to contain lots and lots of disparate views and different groups.' When it came to establishing gate rules about sensitive issues such as mental health, what that constituted and how to handle those exhibiting signs of distress, Alison concluded that 'it's not that straightforward'.

Lyn Barlow also lived at Yellow, having moved there from care at only 17. She recounted the kindness shown to many women with mental health issues. But her personal experience was that 'there was a stigma of mental health [...] while there was this solidarity [...] when it came to like, depression [...] there were women you could tell just couldn't deal with mental health'. Her interviewer asked her if this was a generational issue and she replied: 'Yeah, I think a lot of it was. Because I remember feeling it more from the older women than I did the younger women. And I think as well, that might have been something that was quite particular to Yellow Gate. I don't think maybe that was as evident at other camps.' While she was living there, Yellow – often the seat of heated debates – suffered from a particularly destructive argument between two groups of women which became known as 'the split'. After it, Lyn experienced a different side of camp. 'After the split, I started spending more time at Orange Gate and building relationships with women who lived at Orange [...] who I was in touch with after I left Greenham. Some supported me through thick and thin after Greenham.'

Certainly the size and scale of Greenham's nearly twenty-year life as a peace camp allowed many women to weave themselves into its tapestry, adding their own colour, texture, tale to the growing web. 'Every woman there was different, their needs were different,' said Sue. 'The way that they managed being in Greenham was different. Some people would manage it by staying for two weeks, going away for a couple of days, and coming back. Some people would manage it by staying for months, some people would manage it by doing a demo every day, and going backwards and forwards to jail and to prison.'

Maggie told us it was like 'an open university for women', recalling, 'I remember sitting around some of the fires and just hearing ideas and concepts that I'd never heard before. I mean, it just completely opened me up to so many things.'

While a big action might see hundreds or even thousands of people coming to Greenham, and weekends might swell the overnight residents, much day-to-day time at the camp was often spent with smaller groups of women forming a presence outside the base. As Yellow had the only water spout and the weather regularly made dry wood a rare commodity, especially in winter, simple-seeming chores like making cups of tea and keeping the campfires burning required attention and were time consuming. What this created, however, was the environment and opportunity for in-depth conversation and discussion. While waiting on the fire to heat the kettle or overseeing the safety of their sleeping sisters through the night, women shared experiences, made connections and deconstructed norms, assumptions and prejudices – both their own and those of society in general. 'I think we were very consciously trying to be different, have a sort of woman-dominated view of the world,' Becky Griffiths mused. 'A different power structure, trying to make decisions differently, or behave differently, was definitely about female empowerment.' No stone was left analytically unturned, as language, systems, laws and economics came under the women's scrutiny. A lot, they felt, was wrong with the top-down, violent, hierarchical world that men had created and were running. They set about creating an alternative in the peace camp, establishing collective decision making and leaderless action.

'I'd like the camp to be remembered for the way it organised, which was hugely successful,' Janet Smith told us:

> It's the most long run [...] anarchical feminist organisation, which just really worked. And I think that a lot of people are afraid of the word anarchy, but anarchy isn't chaos, it's actually very well organised. But it's about allowing people to generate, it comes from the person and the small group outwards rather than the other direction. So you use everybody's potential, and everybody's ideas and Greenham really demonstrated that that works. It showed what power women can have when they actually get together, and trust each other, and do things.

Some of the things the women organised show the lengths they were able to go to create a supportive society. According to Ray, some of the gates managed to arrange for post to be delivered: 'You could [...] use Blue Gate, Greenham Common, Burys Bank Road as our address.' This meant that women living full time or longer term at the camp could maintain relationships with friends and family, get information about their life at camp to the wider world and sign on for social security. But the camp's efforts to ensure an egalitarian system didn't end there:

> A lot of women [...] signed on in Newbury, or did postal signing on, but a lot of women for various reasons wouldn't be able to sign on – especially if they were underage or escaping domestic violence [...] and so we had camp dole. When we had lots of donations, which were coming from all over the world, we were able to actually support women financially so they had a bit of personal money.

Ray felt that camp dole helped to create 'a sort of [...] level playing field in that actually you can be a very well-off woman with a very wealthy husband and still have no money, you can still experience domestic violence and abuse [...] you may have still experienced child sex abuse, your family might be coercing you into marriage, or shaming you for being a single parent – all those things transcended class because they affect us all'.

We asked Ray how agreements were reached collectively and she answered: 'Well, meetings, you know, there'd be a lot of meetings.' Decisions without leaders, aiming to achieve a group consensus, sometimes across several gates, meant time needed to be given for every woman to have her say. Alison explained: 'Well, with consensus decision making, you're trying to reach an agreement that everybody is comfortable with [...] it can go on for hours and hours and hours, and it can get incredibly heated.'

With donations coming in, multiple gates and women from all classes and backgrounds debating together, money became the subject of some of the longest, most bitterly contested meetings. Hazel outlined the situation to us:

And they were meetings we had every week, where people would come from all the gates because that was how we would collectively decide how we were going to spend whatever funds we had. And to say they were fraught is an understatement, because there was no, there was no organisation, there was no structure, there was no leader, there was no money committee as such, or treasurer, or whatever. So you came to a 'money meeting'. And you stuck your hand up if you wanted some money for something. So it might be, 'I need a hundred quid to print some leaflets', you know, say from the office in Islington. Or it might be, 'I need a hundred quid to buy a camera because I feel like I need to express my photographic instincts'. And the latter kind of request tended to meet some kind of controversy.

And that's when things got really tricky, because the people who tended to ask for a hundred quid to buy a camera or a hundred quid to go on holiday to Greece for a rest or whatever, tended to be people who didn't have funds. And the people who were quite judgemental said, 'No, no, no, no, we must use all our money for printing leaflets and supporting the cause', they tended to be people who could quite happily go out and buy a camera or have a hundred quid holiday in Greece if that's what they felt like. They were intensely difficult money meetings because it wasn't just about how we were going to collectively decide to spend the money. It became kind of value judgements on what people were asking for the money for, it opened up all sorts of interesting stuff, way beyond the initial sort of thing.

Soon, Hazel explained to us, a top limit was agreed:

There was a feeling, which to an extent I shared [...] kind of like, is this actually what – the people who donated this money, and did these fundraisers – is this what they intended the money to be spent on? There were people asking, 'Can I have fifty quid for a new pair of boots?' We just got like, 'Yes, we're all living in the mud. You can't afford a pair of boots.' Of course, donations are meant to buy a new pair of boots. But when it escalated – 'Can I have six hundred quid to go on a two-week holiday?' – it's like, hang on a minute! Is this really what the people who raised the money were intending it to be spent on? And that's why I think there was a kind of top limit set.

Sue told us that women took it in turns to run the money meetings, at least in the camp's early days. She remembered:

The money meetings [...] depending on who was running them, they went well or badly! I would say that I loved certain people being at the money meetings, because they would stretch out the hand of love and recognise that some women needed different things, other than boots, to make them happy. And I think that was helpful. If you'd like me to be more specific than that, I would probably say the money meeting that I enjoyed the most was when I actually got a pair of boots that I desperately needed. I also got two bars of chocolate that I really wanted. Other women pooled together and went and got weed, and that was really appreciated because we'd had a really hard time, and it was cold, and it was wet, and we were all depressed, and other women were really quite happy to go and get a bottle of booze, or go to the pub, but some of us wanted weed [...] And there was awful trouble the next day about that money meeting. Because all these things were spent, and [...] they would come and tell us, 'That's not a valid thing', but we'd already got our weed, we'd got our chocolate, I'd got my boots.

Arguably one of the camp's greatest strengths was its refusal to elect representatives or leaders. 'It was leaderless, and that really confused the authorities,' stated Carolyn Francis. 'Yeah 'cause they're like, if they can get hold of this one woman, it will stop.' But as each gate, and each individual woman, was responsible for their, or her own, actions, there was no single head to cut off and scupper the organisation, and no overarching secret plans to be discovered by undercover police. 'So it wouldn't matter how much got messed up,' said Hannah Schafer, 'because it couldn't really mess it up [...] obviously there was people who were seen as leaders by the media and things, but you know, there was lots of us there [...] and so all the actions were all just spontaneous [...] there wasn't like a policy to be leaked, or a strategy. So how could you manipulate it? You couldn't!'

Much of camp life was spent in communal food preparation, childcare and conversation. Friends of the photographer's here include Barbara Tombs with her baby Ellen and, in the background on the right, Ruth Green. (Gini Mags)

Though some women feel sure that the camp was subject to 'spy cops' and *agents provocateurs* there to provoke discord, the sheer scale of the camp and its gates often protected it from collapse. Without mobile phones or email, Hazel pointed out that 'discussions would take place at one gate that people at another gate wouldn't necessarily even be aware were happening'. This might make for a longer meeting when groups got together, but it prevented other gates being negatively impacted by events like the split that at one point immobilised the population at Yellow Gate.

In the jovial spirit of non-confrontation, Sue reflected: 'I think there were some people who believed that they were leaders. And that was okay. Because the rest of us thought, "you enjoy that [...] we'll get on with the business of developing ourselves as women, and being as awkward as we can in our demonstrations".'

During her stay at Yellow, Sue, as a Black woman living at camp, was aware of the different treatment she received from the authorities to her white counterparts; she described being given sentences that were twice the length of white Greenham women for the same actions, and being called 'a nigger' by police during arrests. Institutional racism made living conditions at camp even more challenging for women of colour, which some women felt became a catch-22 situation. 'I can understand why lots of Black women came and went, "This is not for us",' Penny told us. 'It was very white.' To try to address this, and keen to learn from and generate an international sisterhood, the Greenham camp reached out to women engaged in similar struggles across the globe. Ray explained:

We were internationally linking with women in Namibia, the Western Shoshone people – there was a women's peace camp at Nevada test site, and the women's peace camp there was on Shoshone land, and the tests were being done on Indian reservation land, and the women's peace camp there had their own bit of land, because in America the arresting thing is so much harder. Women from Greenham went, you know, to the Nevada test site. We paid for women to come from the South Pacific Islands, to come on speaking tours about the sea-testing. There was a women's peace camp at Hiroshima. And right at the beginning of Greenham a woman from there came and lived at Greenham. She died at Greenham of cancer. Hiro, I think she was called.

3

IT AIN'T JUST THE WEB, IT'S THE WAY THAT WE SPIN IT

Creating a women-only space

KATE KERROW

It ain't just the web
It's the way that we spin it,
It ain't just the world
It's the women within it.
It ain't just the struggle
It's the way that we win it.
That's what gets us by.

From 'That's What Gets Us By', *The Greenham Songbook*

'I loved the stimulation of sitting there around the campfire, listening to women talk about their experiences, which were so different from mine. You know, there were women from very, very poor backgrounds who had had horrendous situations while growing up. There were children who'd been beaten by their fathers, or their husbands (…) There were women of such variety there, women with emotional damage (…) women who were on fire, who were there in the centre of their woman-ness, and ready to share it, and ready to show you that there was another way – even if it wasn't for you, showing you another way kind of opens up that narrow perspective that we have. That this is our own life.'

Sue Say

Until second-wave feminism, very little had changed for women in political, social and economic terms since the first wave – that of Suffrage, and its ultimate success in 1928.[9] Between 1918 and 1983, women made up less than 8 per cent of Labour candidates and less than 5 per cent of Conservative,[10] so they were woefully under-represented in Parliament. Women still suffered limits on which jobs they could apply for, and made up a much lower percentage of university students. They were underpaid, domestic violence was rife and marital rape wouldn't be against the law until 1994.[11]

The second wave developed huge momentum during the seventies, with some serious wins for women. In 1971, the first Women's Liberation march took place in London; in 1974, contraception became available through the National Health Service; in 1975, the Sex Discrimination Act was passed; in 1976, several pieces of legislation were achieved that at least attempted to protect women from domestic violence; and, though problematic in a vast number of ways, in 1979 Margaret Thatcher became the UK's first female prime minister (arguably, and ironically, a development that required the help of the feminists she so abhorred; they created a context in which her success was possible).[12] Needless to say, attitudes were still traditional. According to a survey on British Social Attitudes, in the mid 1980s, almost half of the public agreed that 'a man's job is to earn money; a woman's job is to look after the home and family'.[13]

It was in this context that many women came to Greenham – not just to campaign against the holding of nuclear weapons at the common, but to escape the fear and discrimination that was at the centre of their domestic living under the patriarchy. Lynette Edwell was a long-term Greenham woman whose Newbury home was the dedicated 'Greenham Office'. She operated an open-house policy for the women, where they could conduct their campaign (or personal) admin, shower, rest, keep warm and engage in discussions which echoed the phrase repeated by so many of the Greenham women we interviewed: *The personal is political.* 'People would sit around here and have endless conversations about feminism, lesbianism, ending relationships [...] all sorts of things were debated here,' Lynette said. 'I learned more about incest, domestic violence.'

Young women bonded in their defiance of their government's nuclear policy. (Bridget Boudewijn)

Penny Gulliver commented on how widespread women's stories of suffering male violence were at camp:

> [There were] people saying for the first time, 'I've never told anybody about this, but I was sexually abused', and then half the people in the bender would go, 'so was I, so was I' [...] an eighty-year-old woman sat there going, 'My father sexually abused me, and it's the first time that I've told anybody.' [...] Understanding how it fits into the big picture was really powerful in the same way that taking action made you brave. You knew that you could change things.

Many women emphasised how crucial it was for them to be in the company of other women to be able discuss the real and frightening issues that affected their lives – issues that were so connected to male privilege. Debating these topics involved creating safe spaces where women were free to criticise the structures of patriarchy without the potentially silencing constraints of male presence.

It's also important to note that, between 1982 and 1983, there were around twelve other permanent mixed peace camps in the UK, located near to nuclear or US Air Force bases. These included Upper Heyford, Lakenheath, Daws Hill, Molesworth, Wethersfield, and Faslane in Scotland. These peace camps were all open to male supporters. Additionally, at Greenham, Fenja Hill commented that men 'were never made to feel not welcome in the daytime'.

The reticence from some women to send male friends and lovers away from camp may go some way to explain why men appeared to be living at the camp up until February 1982, half a year after the first meeting and the vote on making Greenham women-only. Fran De'Ath, who moved to the camp in its first few weeks with her then-boyfriend, told a story that illustrates how those who didn't support the move towards a women-only Greenham sometimes subverted or ignored the majority decision: 'So these three young lads turned up in the cold, the wet, the dark, and they were only 16 or 17 years old, you know, they were just boys. They didn't know it had gone women-only.' Fran went on to find the boys a space for their tent behind some bushes and to sneak them supper from the communal campfire. She remembers that 'the next morning, all hell was let loose' when the boys were discovered.

It is also possible that men initially refused to leave the camp and abide by the majority wishes of the meetings. While many quietly packed up and moved their work for peace down the road to Aldermaston, several women reported a continued male presence for the first few months, despite the discussion already having taken place about the camp being women-only. When asked how men reacted to being asked to leave, Lynette told us that 'the men were furious, lots of sulking and tantrums'. In her opinion, 'the men that stayed tended to be out-of-work men who were dossing around'.

Many accounts described poor behaviour from the men who were initially welcomed at the site. Peggy Seeger affirmed the women's dissatisfaction: 'At the beginning there were men [...] the men sat around, a lot of them didn't do a bloody thing [...] women tried to tidy up [...] the men lounged for the most part.' Lyn Barlow commented that: 'There was a lot of opposition [...] They saw it as a direct threat to their masculinity, their patriarchal beliefs and values. It really questioned patriarchy, I think, in this country, for probably the first time since the Suffragettes.' Elizabeth Beech described the women's desire for a break from gender-stereotypical roles: 'Our hope was that men would understand that, you know, their role on this occasion was to keep the home fires burning. Women had done that for generations.'

None of this is to say there weren't accounts of the varied and positive contributions from male supporters of Greenham, some of whom also helped us to trace the women and aid the preservation of their political contributions in history. However, given that the majority of women wanted Greenham to be women-only, for reasons that were central to what they were trying to achieve with NVDA and for the purpose of exploring a way of living which liberated them from the oppression they found in their real worlds, the fight against the majority decision does echo the misogynistic attitudes of the time – especially when we consider that there were several mixed peace camps to visit across the UK. The verbal and physical abuse the women received as a result of their choice to create and maintain a women-only camp would continue across their campaign.

Subversive, female-centric art was a regular part of the Greenham women's depiction of their movement. (Jenny Engledow)

Josetta Malcolm went to Greenham at 18 years of age, in 1986. They stayed there until 1988 and largely resided at Blue Gate, having grown up in a relatively strict Jamaican household which resulted in their running away to live at the camp. Josetta is now non-binary, but of the past, they told us: 'I'd had no freedom and I didn't feel very empowered as a woman. I'd been the victim of various kinds of abuse and was quite scared, and had mental health problems.'

Josetta described the impact of going into a space that supported women with mental health problems, that supported women just for being women, as 'everything!'. It gave them 'a language and a political understanding, and a realisation that this is patriarchy – this isn't just me having a difficult childhood'.

In our conversations, they tied their revelatory experience directly to the camp being women-only:

It was like therapy, it was like a political awakening [...] these amazing strong women from all around the world [...] to just see how things linked up, that there was something linked up about patriarchy, and nuclear arms, and war and to make those connections was really quite amazing. To realise that patriarchy is violent and that it's about male violence – and what happens to me, and what happens to lots of women is male violence, and that's about patriarchy [...] It isn't down to an individual not being able to help themselves, or being a bit messed up – it's actually part of a structural system. And I think when you understand that, and then when you meet lots of other women, and you're in a space where it's safe – we get heard, and we get to talk about it.

I think a lot of politics, and a lot of alternative and activist kind of politics are very dominated by men, and Greenham was my first realisation and awakening that women can be strong and powerful, and are clever and have the answers [...] and trying to work things out is better than being adversarial, and using violence creates more violence, and that we can be pacifists in our approaches [...] I know a lot of the impetus of Greenham being women-only was because of all the sexual assaults that still happen in mixed peace camps and mixed spaces. Actually to be in a women-only space and then have your voice heard as a woman is so empowering, because men still take over, men still mansplain, they still dominate, you know – activist spaces are still quite male-dominated which is very sad – all these years later.

The personal benefits of women-only space were directly connected to what many of the women described as 'a feeling' which only came into being when women joined together in male absence. Fenja Hill stated that 'the dynamic is always different when there are men there. I mean, it's not about whether they're good or bad men, but any group of women on their own, and any group of men on their own, will be different if they're mixed because we respond to one another differently.' Peggy Seeger felt similarly: 'Women do things differently, we are different from men [...] When a man turns up [...] it's like a drop of oil in the water, it's a stone that ripples out, even if it's a man that's just trying like hell to fit in [...] Going to Greenham really gave me my first taste of what women can do when we get together.'

Women talked of finding enfranchisement in their new home, not just because they were now outdoors, but because of a new collectivism. Jill 'Ray' Raymond, when showing us some of the Greenham diaries, discussed a 'bleeding chart diary'. 'Everyone filled in their thing on their moon day, when we were bleeding, because we heard about this "If you're in this together, you all bleed together" – it was just an experimental thing,' she said, referencing the common belief that when women live together, or are in regular close contact, their menstrual cycles fall into sync. Smiling, she added: 'We all ended up bleeding at the same time – so we were all pissed off at the same time!' Fenja told us about the 'knicker bush [...] after we washed our knickers out, we used to hang them all over this bush to dry. And there was a bush that was covered in toothpaste because that's where everyone used to clean their teeth and spit on the bush.' Elizabeth felt that the authorities 'really disliked us living our lives in public [...] the domestic was all too visible.' She believed the authorities found it difficult to see what they deemed as 'hordes' of women living their daily lives in full view.

This new way of being, and the women-led nature of it, was illustrated by some of the women's discussions about building shelters or treehouses on the site. A large treehouse was designed and built by

Interviewee Jenny Engledow showing a peace banner to her interviewer, Kate Kerrow. (Christine Bradshaw)

a group of women with the aim of being occupied by them during the first eviction. The walls were woven out of reed, and the aim was to avoid putting even a single nail into the tree; such an act was seen by these women as a disruption to nature, as an action that could cause harm. This moving example of the all-nurturing way women were working for peace at the nuclear base is echoed in Maggie Parks's account of her spiritual experience at Embrace the Base in December 1982. 'In a very sort of magical way, it was this huge energy circle of women. And I think it was that moment of that energy circling thirty thousand women that was so life-changing for many of us, even though we had no sort of conscious knowledge of it. I think something extremely amazing and magical, and for me spiritual, I think, happened – although I didn't know it at the time.'

Josetta referenced the impact of the inter-generational learning between the women in this new space. 'From a woman called Mel who lived in Newbury [...] who taught us car mechanics, to practical stuff – the woman bringing food to us, to all the stories, to the international connections and connections between our campaigns [...] just generally meeting and being inspired by lots of old women – women of all ages.' They also felt the political awakening around feminism opened their eyes to race politics, despite Greenham being largely white: 'I came across people like Audre Lorde, and Toni Morrison – lots of Black women, and Black lesbians [...] I came across Black women's writing and politics at Greenham.'

The life-changing learning emerged in a myriad of ways. Women, liberated by the absence of men, found themselves, often for the first time, falling in love with other women. Lyn Barlow discussed how it transformed her understanding of how her personal life intersected with her transforming political views:

In care, I'd gravitated towards boys because I'd been badly bullied by a lot of the girls [...] So I'd never done anything women-only, but always had a healthy disrespect for male authoritarian figures because they reminded me of my father [...] So Greenham, it challenged me, because I was, on the one level, really drawn to the fact that it was women-only [...] But I was afraid at the same time because of my previous experiences of being bullied by girls [...] I guess I'd been a closet feminist in my childhood and this was first time that I'd actually understood what feminism was really about. And how the personal is political, and joining up the dots between things that happened to me in my childhood, and poverty, and working-class roots, unemployment – it all made more sense once I'd become involved with Greenham.

The benefits of the camp being women-only weren't just centred around the personal development of the women, however. The women were developing campaign strategies, pushing forward revolutionary methods of protest in their use of NVDA. One of the key factors in the decision to make the camp women-only was the concern that men would be counterproductive and hinder the creation of a non-violent campaign.

'To do blockades, totally non-violently, is much easier as women-only [...] if there had been men it would have probably been worse because

Women often used this method of blockading, sometimes called a 'die-in', to obstruct the base. (Janet Smith)

it would have ended up with a big fight,' said Ray. This was echoed by Fenja: 'Not for all men, but it is more of a male response to a perceived threat, is violence.' Elizabeth believed that while men often *felt* they were being supportive, it was hard for them to recognise when they were being aggressive. 'It's very difficult to maintain non-violence in mixed groupings,' she said. 'There is also the violence within ourselves in terms of our thoughts and how we might be subconsciously acting on that a lot of the time.'

Jenny Engledow, who lived at and visited Greenham throughout its entire nineteen-year history, felt that there was a fear of triggering testosterone: 'Then there would be more potential for violence, and aggression, and even verbal aggression [...] women had a very clear way of not wanting to engage [...] always trying to lower the anger and keep things to a minimum.' Fenja believed the women-only rule actually served to protect the campaigners themselves: 'Some of the squaddies wouldn't want to hit a woman so they were more careful about violence [...] it was probably less violent because there were no men.'

Fenja also acknowledged that many women wouldn't have come unless it was women-only, in part because they wouldn't have felt safe at night. The sprawling camp was dark and unforgiving, and there are a significant number of testimonies detailing the violence the women experienced from outsiders who broke into the camp; understandably, the women wanted to protect themselves. 'We wanted to feel safe at night,' Fenja explained. 'And I suppose lots of women wouldn't have.' Vicki Smith, a member of Cruise Watch who regularly stayed at Greenham, reflected on the idea of safety at night and the camp being women-only. 'I was absolutely fascinated by this as an idea, and of course it was a time when women were really quite vulnerable on the streets. I remember having to be very, very careful,' she told us. 'Just the idea of camping out at night in a women-only space was very attractive to me personally.'

By actively claiming space as women-only, the women rejected passivity; they became the decision-makers. 'Men have a tendency to want to be in charge,' Fenja stated. 'The authorities never quite got to grips with the non-hierarchical thing, but it was much easier to try and persuade them of that when it was all-women.' Recognising that the presence of men would have made the dynamic very different, she told us: 'The people on the inside of the fence would have looked to the men, would have asked them the questions and would have assumed that the men were in control.' Ray talked about how the women navigated this perception with the journalists who visited: 'Three men would come with cameras and all this equipment, and they'd go, "Oh, can we speak to – who's in charge around here? Can we speak to the leader?" and we'd say, "Oh no, we don't have leaders [...] When you send a woman to come and interview us, if you're lucky you'll get an interview".' Acknowledging that at that time there weren't many women photographers or journalists, Ray remembered thinking, 'Give a woman a job, you know?'

Mica May shared an anecdote about her experiences with other activists:

I remember speaking to people from Greenpeace, who said, 'You know, it's only ever the men who get to do any of the radical actions' [...] We did go and visit Faslane, and spoke to a woman who was there,

83

and the way she was talking it was clear it was the men who did every-thing [...] She was really curious about how we were able to decide things, and have the people who wanted to do something, do it, and the people who didn't want to do it, didn't have to do it. And the ones who didn't do it, they didn't have to be the bottle-washers either.

Elizabeth remembered how, at Embrace the Base, the men were asked to make sandwiches for the women. 'They got an inordinate amount of praise for making these sandwiches,' she said. 'I refused to take part in it.' Claiming Greenham as a women-only space, and reversing gender stereotypes by placing men into support roles, meant the women had the chance to truly lead themselves according to their own value systems.

Alison Napier worked in mental health services after Greenham. Reflecting upon the aims of Greenham to be a safe space for all women, she recognises how women with mental health problems, rejected in society for difficult behaviour, were welcomed at camp, and allowed to become the leaders of their own lives. Their active part in the community resulted in exploratory debate of issues surrounding mental health.

'I can look back and I can identify specific individuals who were clearly what we would call not well,' Alison explained, telling us:

I think Greenham was a place where people who, in another context – their behaviour, their views could be seen as problematic – were just able to be absorbed [...] It could be a safe place for women who just wanted to be away from mainstream life for a little while [...] There were a couple of people there with severe mental health problems, and again polarised views would happen – some people were think-ing, 'This woman is clearly very ill, we maybe need to get her to a hospital', and somebody else would be saying, 'She just needs a safe place – somewhere to speak and talk and be listened to'.

The polarisation of views often led to discussion of, and thereby engagement with, the complexity of the situations faced by those who suffered poor mental health. This engagement led to empathy and action; Yoko Ono gave money to the women, and, though not confirmed, some say this money was used to buy a small area of land near to the base and provide a caravan. This would act as a sanctuary and a place for the women to go to for privacy when they were unwell, either physically or mentally.

Sue Say seconded that there was a desire for a learning-based approach when supporting women with mental health problems:

There were some people who were very vulnerable at camp. And there were some issues that came up that were interesting to explore. And we had a woman called Metal Carol – every part of her body had bits of metal stuck through it. She had an affinity with metal [...] But there was a big debate at one point about her legitimacy for being there [...] Women were very uncomfortable about looking at the idea of 'Hold on a minute, who do you think you are to decide who can be at camp and who can't?' [...] There became meetings and discussions about things that actually were nobody's goddamn business, there were public meetings about people's relationships [...] but it was good to see where people thought the lines were.

Several women discussed the considerable pressure on the camp to carefully manage women who were unwell and were rejected by outside society. 'We had some women at Blue Gate that were really mentally unwell,' Ray said. 'It was very difficult because we didn't want to be handing them over to the state, but knowing how to support them when you're struggling with the conditions and everything was difficult as well [...] They'd wander off at night, they'd disappear for days, and we didn't know where they'd be [...] I mean, it was really scary.'

Penny also told us how responsible the women felt for the more vulnerable women at camp. 'There was one woman with quite severe mental health problems, and it was quite stressful [...] She was wanting to keep warm [...] we nicked a bit of the council fence and we burned it [...] We never did things like that – we never touched council property, but that time we did – we took a bit of that old fashioned twisty wooden fence, and the soldier rung it in, and the police arrived and arrested us.' Penny revealed that their arrests resulted in the woman being left by herself, not safeguarded. The police failed to respond to the woman's needs, and her being left in solitude for that period of time was reportedly 'a disaster'.

Sue said she left before the split of the camp, but she noted that the split changed Greenham in terms of how it operated as a safe space for women:

> I left when women were loving each other [...] and caring for each other, and being furious with each other, and being angry with each other, and being positively awkward at sometimes, because that's what women are [...] Coming back after to see how far away changed my home had become – that it wasn't home any more [...] It wasn't like that before – it was full of love and care, and sharing and giving and compassion and passion.

Sue noted the moment that changed her feelings about Greenham was when she observed a woman being refused water because of a disagreement. 'I reached my hand out for the standpipe and I walked and gave it to that woman [...] and I just thought Greenham is dead. Greenham is dead if you are refusing a woman water – what is wrong with you?'

Echoing the importance of maintaining tolerance, Josetta described one of their key learnings from Greenham as 'your right to be whoever it is you are'. Feeling the seeds for this tolerance were sown in Greenham, they said:

> You know, that's in my DNA [...] There's something unique about Greenham and Greenham women [...] it's now in our DNA – that experience, that knowledge, that learning, that approach to life [...] There are thousands of women who were touched, who either lived there, or who were raised by women who lived there or visited there, or supported it, or knew about it – and I think all of those politics that we talked about came from Greenham [...] we live our lives informed by that.

Feminist symbols, messages and art were regularly woven into the fence surrounding the base. (Linda Broughton)

Peggy felt some of the most powerful learnings she took from Greenham sprang from the women-only dynamic. 'I'd been in a heterosexual marriage for twenty-five years. Our friends were couples [...] I didn't have a group of women friends, most of my life was heterosexual [...] Most of my friends are now older women. I really like being in groups of women.' Peggy now lives with her long-term female partner. Many accounts discussed Greenham as a place which liberated women's desires to be in romantic relationships with women. In this way, and many others, the women-only space at Greenham helped transform women's domestic spheres, often leading to a re-creation of those spheres as women-only spaces, and the removal of the cross-cultural communication struggle between the sexes.

4

WHICH SIDE ARE YOU ON?

Local and national relationships

REBECCA MORDAN

Oh, which side are you on?
Are you on the side of suicide,
Are you on the side of homicide,
Are you on the side of genocide?
Are you on the side that don't like life,
Are you on the side of racial strife,
Are you on the side that beats your wife?
Which side are you on?

From 'Which Side Are You On?', *The Greenham Songbook*

While the Greenham women laughed, loved, argued, sang and struggled making their society at the peace camp, their very existence polarised a watching world. To some, they were inspiring heroines who braved all weathers, increasingly harsh conditions and prison to challenge seemingly insurmountable odds for the good of all life on earth. To others, they were, at best, scruffy, bleeding-heart layabouts, and at worst, deviant miscreants with nefarious, dangerous connections to the Soviets.

The manner in which local and national groups, and individuals, related to the camp and its women reflects the politics of the time. The contexts were the swell of radical feminism in a prevailing tide of patriarchy, the rising awareness of the impending climate crisis and the strong nuclear debate raging throughout the world.

Satire was a valuable tool in the Greenham women's campaign. This poster adapts a classic romance from the golden age of Hollywood cinema to show the relationship between the American president, Ronald Reagan, and the British prime minister, Margaret Thatcher, who worked closely together to push an international pro-nuclear agenda. (Bridget Boudewijn)

'*Greenham Women Are Everywhere* – that was again a non-hierarchical thing. It wasn't like "Oh you're not a real Greenham woman because you don't live here",' Jill 'Ray' Raymond told us, reflecting on one of the famous Greenham mottos. Once Greenham had been established, and it became clear that it was a community with no plans of leaving the common any time soon, a web of support and interest developed that both facilitated the camp and exponentially extended the reach of its messages. As the numbers of people coming to the camp and carrying its stickers, badges and principles away with them increased, it did begin to seem as if there were Greenham women everywhere.

Sally Hay explained: 'The purposes of our visits were to take supplies, and we took probably my own bodyweight in lentils, I should have thought! And warm, dry clothes and wellingtons, and things like that – tinned food, in fact, that's what I remember taking.'

Gillian Booth and Hazel Pegg remembered the women who came from all over the country, bringing food, clothing, period products, sometimes staying for weekends, month after month. Gillian told us that at first 'there was no sort of, you know, hierarchy between the women that were there all the time and the women that came on occasion'. But then she added: 'That's not strictly true – there were parts of the camp who looked down on them as part-timers.' Hazel continued: 'But most of us really appreciated them, even the women who came only for a few hours, they were just as important as we were, hanging out there for months on end. We couldn't have done it without them.' Gillian agreed: 'They were great, they came up to keep their eye on those sleeping and make sure everything was okay at night, so that we could sleep. I was very grateful for that.'

Sally found that her experience of going to camp, while often rewarding and friendly, could sometimes be coloured by certain interactions:

There are certain women who I've experienced as being more judgemental. You know, I had a male partner then [...] the atmosphere was more hostile to women who were in relationships with men, and there's also a slight sort of, 'Well, you're not really committed are you? You come down once a week in your red wellingtons and clutter the place up with your fucking lentil curry!' And I think I felt judged as not quite cool enough.

Perhaps because of this attitude, and in recognition of the gruelling nature of a more permanent life at camp, many women we interviewed who hadn't lived full time at Greenham were keen to stress this to us, being uncomfortable assuming the title of 'Greenham woman' which they felt should be reserved for the camp's residents. But most of those residents that we interviewed categorically ruled out divisions. When asked by her interviewer, 'What is a Greenham woman?', Lorna Richardson told us:

A Greenham woman is any damn woman who wishes to call herself a Greenham woman. And I think it's antithetical to both the spirit and the practicality of Greenham to divide women into camp women who lived there, and visitors who did not [...] And it's funny, the squaddies that we used to know at Emerald had a term they used to call some of the women: SAS – Saturdays and Sundays. But it's a false division, both philosophically and practically [...] there's this amazing, amazing woman who was a retired Catholic school teacher, who drove like a rally driver on speed, who could follow a cruise convoy in the middle of the night like nobody you've ever met in your life, absolutely extraordinary woman, loved her to bits [...] and I'm pretty sure [...] she's exactly the sort of person who'd go, 'Ooh I never lived there'. Yeah, but she was there, over a long period of time, you know, she had a house for us [...]

If you divided Greenham into women who said they lived there, and the women who called themselves supporters, or visitors or any of those other iterations, then Greenham would be a fraction of what it was and it would be lesser [...] it does not reflect the reality of Greenham. Women who spent a short time there either once in their life, or as often as they liked, are every bit as much Greenham women if they choose to be so [...] You know, it's like the women who come up and again, I think a lot of them saw themselves as supporters who would do a night shift, if you're waiting for the convoy or if we were experiencing a lot of attacks [...] You take one part out of it, the rest of it falls apart. All those are part of it, and that whole 'supporters and Greenham women' thing, I think is philosophically and practically untenable. And not helpful. And just not true. You know?

This practice of women staying for shorter stays, often just a night or two, became known as Night Watch and was particularly deployed when women living full time at camp had just come back from an action, court or prison to help them catch up on much-needed rest. Sally was a part of this support system and recalled sitting up for nights around the campfire while 'groups of pissed up men [...] drove past yelling, "Fucking lezzers" at us, and calling us dirty, which given that we're sitting in mud [...] What would you expect I should be wearing? Court shoes and ten denier stockings? I mean, don't be ridiculous.'

Friends Annei Soanes and Margaret McNeill, who lived in nearby Camberley and came to the camp through their local CND, discussed their experiences of being in the Night Watch crew. Margaret recalled:

The first time we went was a night when the women had been arrested. And they all gradually came back to the camp during the day, and they were tired, very tired. And so we would go, in response to that, and guard them for the night. We were guarding the Greenham women so they could sleep, because there were often occasions when they were harassed – either by local people, or by the guards inside. So they couldn't just sleep [...] I remember specifically there was a motorbike drew up quite close. And there were two guys sitting on this motorbike. And suddenly it went very still in the camp, and they were watching. And then a guy put his hand in his pocket, and everybody stiffened. And then he just lit a fag, and off they drove. And I said, 'What was that about?', and they said, 'Well, you just never know. You never know what they're going to do. Whether it's just somebody interested in what's going on, just a sightseer. Or whether that's a bomb in his pocket, and he's gonna chuck it out.' [...]

They just did not know what was going to happen, or whether they'd be attacked in the night. So they were so brave, those women. And I felt in a way, like we were the frauds, because we didn't stay, we didn't live there. We lived near enough so we could visit, and so we used to go in response, and when they needed a hand, and also on the food rotas, as well – especially in winter, when they could do some nice hot food. So we really got into it in that way, and obviously through the big demos, and so we visited them very frequently.

But those women who lived there were amazing [...] and the things they'd sacrificed as well to be there. Just extraordinary. And so to be able to just go there and support them was brilliant.

Annei was 24 when she started going to the camp, working as a beauty therapist in Harrods in the week and then taking off her false eyelashes and gold lamé and going to Greenham at the weekends. Her time at the camp was a consciousness-raising experience that changed the way she perceived herself and her idea of womanhood:

I was going through that whole process of: What does it mean then? What does it mean to be a woman in the world? What does it mean to not be a Conservative with high heels? And whatever else I thought it meant. You know, what is it, what's it like being in the world in a different kind of way? [...] And what that experience of Greenham gave me was an opportunity to learn about myself, and other people [...] after I did that, I went into Harrods on the Monday morning and I handed my notice in.

This sentiment was echoed by Sue Say: 'Greenham was about building, it was about making a difference and working together, and changing the world at the same time as looking at yourself and changing you.'

Many of the women in Night Watch were also in Cruise Watch. As Sue pointed out: 'They were housing these nuclear weapons that were making us a target for other countries to blow the hell out of us.' This concern drew support for the campaign from an alarmed public. Another common fear was that foreign agents, in particular Soviet ones, now had reason to infiltrate the base and steal nuclear codes or state documents, or even use or sabotage the weapons stored there. In response to this, the government argued that Greenham was one of the most well-defended bases in Europe, and that the RAF were able to not only house, but if necessary move and deploy these weapons of mass destruction in the utmost secrecy. Cruise Watch, a hugely successful synergy of Greenham women based at the camp and the wider web of the peace movement, showed the public and the media the problems with this argument: 'When cruise came in on 14 November 1983,' explained Penny Gulliver,

Survivors of the atomic attack on Hiroshima, several of whom visited, lived and campaigned at Greenham. (Dawn Stewart)

'Emerald Gate was set up by a Japanese woman [...] they set up literally on the other side of the fence from the cruise.'

From here, the women could see when the soldiers were getting the missiles ready to take out on convoy – a military exercise which practised moving the missiles to places where they could be deployed if need arose. For those like Penny, living at Blue Gate, it was obvious when the cruise missiles were on the move, as they would come out at their part of the camp:

> And you'd go, 'Oh my god there's loads of police arriving', and it'd be like three in the morning, and you'd go, 'They must be bringing it out', and someone would have to run or cycle to the nearest phone box on the estate to set off the telephone tree – but invariably someone would get to the box and the phone wasn't working, because they used to cut the phone lines at the same time as cruise came out. And there would be like hundreds of police that would surround you, and cruise would come out of Blue Gate [...] that was always in your mind that

you couldn't just skip it and go to sleep, because you were where it was coming out of, and you can imagine they [the women] would have gone mad if we'd let it come out without telling anybody.

Reaching those signed up to Cruise Watch in a time before the internet or mobile phones relied on the 'telephone tree': when the cruise missiles came out, a woman would call one local person, who would call ten other people, who would each call ten other people and so on. Many of those people, after making their calls, would then get into their cars and make their way to the A-roads around the common until the military convoy was spotted. Then these ordinary members of the public, and occasionally some sympathetic journalists, would flank the road, ending all pretence at secrecy for the military manoeuvres, and sharing the information with their networks the next day. Certainly, this made it hard for most people not to ask themselves just how difficult it might really be for highly trained agents of an enemy state to discover vital secrets about some of the most dangerous weapons known to humanity, if a bunch of untrained peaceniks could so easily point to their whereabouts.

Numbers at the camp were often swelled by dozens of local CND groups up and down the country, who supported Cruise Watch, Night Watch and large actions, as well as the day-to-day running of the camp. 'CND gave us endless support,' Ray told us, and a great number of women we interviewed said they arrived at camp through involvement with their local CND group. It was organisations like CND and the Quakers, together with countless individuals, who rallied support for the campaigns, actions and demos by letter. 'If you asked people of the age now that we were then,' said Sally, 'to organise thousands of women to go and hold hands round a facility in Newbury, but [adopting strict voice] "you may only use paper and pen", they'd be like, "No, that is literally impossible!" But it wasn't – it was done by letter.'

Members of the radical artistic and squatting community also threw their weight behind the camp, enlivening demos with music and costume. Jude Munden, who had been lured away from home at 15 after falling in love with a girl she saw busking on the Tube, regularly visited Greenham and other peace camps throughout the UK with the Fall Out Marching Band:

An anti-nuclear street protest band based in London [...] which was my runaway-and-join-the-circus when I was a bad teenager [...] They're fantastic. And one of the most thrilling things about that band is that we still meet and we still play [...] with subsequent generations now. So my kids have played for them. And we meet at WOMAD[14] once a year, and do all the Brexit, anti-Trump, climate change type marches.

Greenham women also made links with socialist and working-class campaigns in the UK, sending the striking miners any non-vegetarian food that they were donated, and in return, the miners sent them coal. The miners' wives also came and stayed at Greenham or visited for actions, and Judy Harris remembered: 'We went to stay in Cardiff for a few weeks [...] and went and picketed at Port Talbot.' Anne Scargill – at the heart of the miners' strikes through connections with her community and nearly forty-year marriage to the president of the National Union of Mineworkers, Arthur Scargill – visited Greenham and was shocked to observe the police pushing the women around there. 'Little did I know,' she said, grimly, 'that years later, we were going to get the same treatment.'

Sometimes help or support came from unlikely sources. Carolyn Francis remembered that Islington Council gave the women a four-storey house: 'I think there was a basement and a kitchen level, and then an office level, and then the top floor was for sleeping, and a little garden out the back. And it was like a London base camp for the Greenham women's movement.' It was while visiting her sister, who was staying at the house for a temporary break from Yellow Gate, that Carolyn was talked into joining the camp:

I was basically making a living busking in North London and then my sister was involved with the Greenham movement and was looking after the Greenham house on a temporary basis. And so I just started to hang out there, and sleep there sometimes [...] And then one time they were gonna have a big discussion – I think they called it a 'corroboree' at Greenham – a decision-making process, everyone just in a big group talking about this, that, the other, like, round a fire, like for as long as it took, you know [...] and then because I played the fiddle,

Women who were involved in the miners' strikes often visited the Greenham women, many of whom reciprocated this support by joining campaigns in the mining communities. (Bridget Boudewijn)

people said to me, 'You must come down and play, because we need music at this thing, we can't just have talk.'

Even more unpredictable affirmation was remembered by Jade Britton, who recounted to us:

One time when it was pouring with rain and nobody felt like getting out of the van at all, because it was just mud everywhere, somebody knocked on the van, and we reluctantly opened the door, and they said, 'Oh we've got these women here from Bulgaria, and they want to talk to you.' And we said, 'You know, it's not a good day – take them round to Orange Gate, because they've got tarpaulins and they can sit out there and it'll be warm, because they've got a fire – we haven't even got a fire going.' So they went off, and Elizabeth, who was one of the women at Violet Gate, she said, 'Oh I'm going to go off,' because she had her own car, and she said, 'I'm going to go off and see about this.' Anyway, she came back about three hours later [...] and she was twirling something in her hand, and I said, 'What's that?' And she said, 'Oh, it's a medal – it's the highest honour you can give to a woman in Bulgaria, and they were handing them out to Orange Gate' [...] and it was like okay, well we missed that one, but never mind.

Visitors were often seen as a mixed bag. Sometimes the road to inconvenience for a Greenham woman could be paved by friendly intentions. Penny told us that 'men would turn up, and you'd say, "It's okay, come over to the fire, where have you come from?", and then he'd go, "You know what you're doing is wrong", and you'd go, "For fuck's sake!"'. A regular criticism Penny remembered from male visitors was 'you're a bit untidy', to which the women would often point out, 'Well, that's because the police or bailiffs have been through and wrecked everything.' Penny gave such comments short shrift, telling the visitor that 'sometimes that's not the priority – tidying up. I know you think that's what women should be doing, but it's not a priority.'

There was also sometimes a discrepancy between the reality of life at Greenham and the perception a visitor might have of the camp, or indeed, the expectation they had for their visit. The fact that the gates were scattered around the base and had different characters and population sizes was not something that came across from a media interested mainly in sensational stories and a few key spokeswomen. According to Jade, to a lot of visitors 'Yellow Gate was the activist gate and the political gate, because that's where all the cameras went [...] I mean it did wind me up terribly one time.' She went on to explain:

> I went to stay at Red Gate one time and a lot of people had gone off for various things, I think there were only two of us that were there, and when we woke up at like half five or six in the morning, the police had arrived with the bailiffs and the munchers ready to tear down everything. And a woman in a very expensive sports car rolled up, and she said, 'Oh, I'm looking for the Greenham women, I want to know if they need any help?' And I said, 'Well, as you can see, we're getting evicted, and there's only two of us, so we can't rescue everyone's things, and if you can help that would be wonderful', and she kind of looked us up and down, and she said, 'No, actually I was wanting to go and speak to the *real* Greenham women'. I said, 'Well, you want Yellow Gate, then – you just keep on going, love,' and off she went, roared away and left us to it [...] She wanted the place where all the campers were, because that's what she thought was the 'real' camp.

But Jade also remembered 'the incredible generosity of people who would just turn up, and you know you might never seem them again'. One night, after the first big eviction that she experienced, she told us that 'they had taken away a lot of equipment the women had been using, and the benders and things', which meant that until those items could be replaced, 'obviously you were sleeping outside before you could come up with anything else to cover you or to sleep in'. To try to protect themselves from the cold, the women would put their sleeping bags into plastic bags 'but the condensation is terrible, and you end up wringing wet', so soon they started to try to find breathable Gore-Tex bags:

> And people were saying, 'Oh you know, we tried to get Gore-Tex bags, but we couldn't get them anywhere, we were trying in London and all the shops were saying they were sold out.' I can remember a guy

coming down and he opened the boot of his car and he said, 'How many of you are staying here, how many of you need Gore-Texes?' And we were all like putting our hands up, and he was literally handing them out like packets of crisps, and in those days they were really expensive [...] he must have gone out and bought up everything he could find.

As the camp developed, attracting more people and an increasingly hostile press, relationships with those close to Greenham and its women intensified. Penny remembered:

Hideous stuff in the press constantly [...] there were blokes in drive-bys at Blue Gate all the time, people got beaten up – some people got beaten up when they were arrested. Things were thrown at you – I remember a farmer coming by and just shooting pig shit over everybody. Biscuit tins of blood, that kind of thing. So they were endless, those things. But it was a bit like, well, you know, you had a make-do wash under a bucket somewhere, and you carried on.

Still, families were torn between those who followed their wives, mothers, sisters and daughters into supporting the camp, and those who closed the doors on their departing womenfolk in rage and disgust. The military towns that housed the majority of the population around Greenham – Newbury and Thatcham close by, and Farnham, Camberley and more stretching out in increasing circles from the common – were no less extreme in their reactions. 'The base provided money for the town,' Hazel Pegg explained. 'It provided employment. We were not welcomed by the majority of locals. We were dirty, smelly, constantly smelled of smoke. We were a bunch of lesbian hippies. And we brought unwanted press attentions there and arrests; they were living in a nice quiet little market town. They didn't want all this stuff going on.'

Most locals confined their displeasure to writing stern letters to the papers and their councillors, and banning anyone suspected of being a Greenham woman from shops, cafes and pubs. The nearby Little Chef adopted this policy, only for the whole chain then to be subjected to a nationwide boycott in solidarity with the camp. Suddenly, its doors opened again, allowing the women the cooked breakfasts that helped sustain them during the wet and cold months at camp.

Gillian Booth described how trips into town became increasingly 'tricky' and added, 'I used to get spat on.' And others took their negativity even further. Ray talked about the importance of Night Watch 'because of the vigilantes'. We asked her if the vigilantes were local residents and she replied, 'Some of them were out of uniform squaddies as well.'

Hazel and Gillian recalled one particularly alarming night when vigilantes set fire to the gorse that ran around the women's tents. 'That was dodgy,' Gillian commented grimly. After that, she remembered: 'I always kept my clothes on on a Saturday night cause we were in these benders and they could have tossed anything in there and burned you to death [...] you might need to make a quick exit.'

We asked Sarah Green, who was living at Yellow Gate with her young son, if she encountered any of the local vigilantes and she replied: 'Yes, I was there at a time when a car, a sort of van lorry thing-y pulled up and just spread – it was offal. All over, all over.'

But many local residents took a very different approach. Hazel remembered the people living near the camp who would open up their houses 'to let us go and have showers [...] we were over there having showers all the time, to put clothes in the washing machine.'

Judy had similar memories of gratitude:

There was women who lived mostly in Newbury, or some in Thatcham, I think, who were like bath women, and our bath woman was called Audrey [...] And she'd make sure there was hot water, and we'd go to the laundrette and wash everything. And then we'd go and have a bath, and then we'd have clean clothes to put on. And she used to give us a cup of tea and that – I don't think she was in any peace groups or anything.

Other women remembered the ways locals sometimes showed support, not through political affinity but as interested individuals. Jade shared the following anecdote with its clash of cultures:

I was taking driving lessons while I was down there with another woman, and we had this lovely guy – he was an older guy from

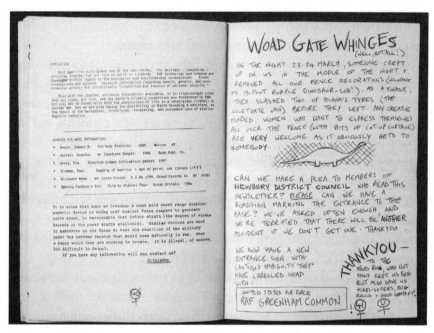

Extensive communal diaries were kept by different gates with various residents taking it in turns to record their thoughts, experiences and communications. (Jenny Engledow)

Thatcham, and he was really retired, but that was his contribution to the effort, giving us driving lessons. And we were driving one day, and we were going along, and I went, 'Oh my god, look! There's a muncher at Blue Gate', and he said [*affecting a slightly posh voice*], 'Uh, sorry are we supposed to do something?' I said, 'Yes, we need to turn around and go back and warn the other gates because everybody is asleep', and he went, 'Okay Jade, if you could just take a right here', and so we turned around and drove back. And he stopped opposite Violet Gate and he went, 'What do we do now?' And I went, 'Just roll the window down and shout, "Munchers at Blue Gate!", okay', and he went, 'Oh, okay then [*clears throat*], Munchers at Blue Gate!' and he rolled it up and says, 'Do we go to another one now?' I said, 'Yeah, we'll go to Orange Gate!'

Some of the most consistent support the women received was from the Newbury Quakers, who, as Gillian described to us, faced 'the wrath of their fellow citizens to host Greenham'. She went on: 'They let us play the movie *Carry Greenham Home* [...] and we could go there and stay [...] They supported us hugely, hugely. And I thought they were very brave. Yeah, incredibly brave.'

Ray summed up the situation in her account of the women's relationship with Newbury:

We were banned from everywhere in Newbury, except the Quakers [...] In the end, they turned over their meeting hall, which was right next to Newbury bus station, which was fantastic because women would get off the bus, quite disorientated with all these bags, and they installed a shower and a washing machine and a dryer. Because drying things was a nightmare. And we could have meetings there if we were planning NVDA [...] we could talk there, so that was a really supportive thing. And there was one cafe called the Empire Grill which would let us in. Because we did stink, you couldn't really not stink [...] So yeah, we were banned from everywhere except the Empire Grill, which was quite near the bus station, and the Quaker meeting house.

The women shared the common with even closer neighbours: there were daily interactions between the MoD police and the British soldiers and rarer encounters with the Americans nestled in the heart of the base. Sally Hay remembered how the Americans would:

Often come to the fence and you'd be there with your bolt-cutters trying to cut the fence and they'd sort of go [*adopting an American accent*], 'Oh geez man, please don't do that'. And we would say, 'Well, we need to come in there, it's common land. And we think you've got something really big and dangerous in there, and we need to get it off the common land because it is dangerous.' And then they'd say, 'You know I can bring the police to come down and arrest you.' And women [...] would say, 'All right, but if you could just hold the wire tight, because it's easier to snip', and you know, generally take the piss. I can't see a pair of wellingtons these days – even now after all these years – without wondering if they're wide enough to get my leg and the bolt-cutters in them.

But women who lived longer term at the camp often found the Americans were the hardest to engage with. 'You never saw the Americans, because they kept separate from that,' Jade told us. 'Occasionally there would be one of them, an American would drive up, and get out, and talk, and the British squaddies were like, "Okay mate, you've been here twenty minutes, if you're here any longer we're going to have to report you", and we'd always say, "Go now, because we don't want you to get into trouble", and stuff like that.' We asked her if she could remember any particular conversations, and she said that the personnel who made those kind of visits 'were concerned about the whole nuclear idea'.

Margaret McNeill remembered:

Even then I didn't feel anti-military, I felt that people who were in the military were people of honour, they were holding those roles because they did care about people and their country. And I actually felt angry on their behalf, because I felt they were having to defend something that was morally wrong. And they had no power in that [...] I remember the first night I was there, because I'd never been, and it was dark by the time we got there. And so I thought, 'Well, I'll just go along and see what the fence is like.' So I walked along the fence [...] and I suddenly realised to my horror that there was a guy inside shadowing me with his rifle [...] and at first I was quite frightened. So I sort of scuttled back to our crowd and then I thought this is laughable, this poor chap is reduced to stalking this middle aged woman! You know, because I might be a threat to him and his bombs.

Lorna Richardson chose Greenham over A levels in 1982 when she was 17, helping to set up Emerald Gate and living for a time at Green, then Yellow and finally Blue, the gate for which she had 'a soft spot the size of the Albert Hall'. She had regular interactions with soldiers in her migration around the camp: 'They would be so bored. Very, very, very bored indeed. And they'd talk to you [...] they were desperate for a chat and they'd occasionally be posted singly or sometimes they'd sort of do a joint shift together [...] they were probably my age, you know [...] I was very young. They were very young, a lot of them.' She recounted two in particular who 'didn't know how to make a fire. You know, it's snowing and they've got [...] braziers [...] And so we'd throw them over kindling.' In return for this help:

A sweet couple of lads said, 'Do you want some coal?' And we were like, sure why not? And so, bless them, they had this army-issue coal, they tried to throw a bag of coal over the fence. And of course, it's quite a high fence and they've got three rolls of barbed wire on the top and it catches in the barbed wire. And so it drops down. It's now full of little tiny holes. And so they go, 'Oh that's not gonna work. Why don't you cut a hole in the fence?' And we go, 'All right then!' And there's literally snow on the ground. So we cut a hole in the fence and they shove it through the hole. And we just sort of, you know, pull the fence back to where it was. And we went by the silos. And because the coal bag now has little holes in it, there's this sort of little trail of coal dust to this badly-put-together hole in the fence.

Many women felt it was part of their commitment to NVDA to break down this 'us and them' mentality, trying to develop human connection and empathy with those guarding the base. Maria Ragusa remembered that:

At Violet Gate, you made it a policy to always try to talk to anybody that was to do with the police, the military – communicate with them [...] give them a little bun or something, and then have a little chat with them [...] Sometimes, I'd say, 'Well, what do you think about this, then?', 'Oh I think it's pointless.' 'Oh, okay then, so that's interesting, what do you think should happen? Are you for nuclear war, do you think it's a good idea? How would you feel about us using a nuclear weapon against another country with the possibility they might retaliate? What do you think about that?' It was called Subversion by Tea!

Jade had a similar memory of how 'one of our women ended up writing to a squaddie for quite a long time' after chatting to him through the fence day after day. Connections could be made that were moving for both parties. Gillian recalled asking a British serviceman she spoke to regularly:

'How long have you been doing this?' [...] And he said he'd done active service [...] And I said, just came out with it, I said, 'Have you ever killed anyone?' And it was a huge silence. And then he said, 'Yes.' I said, 'Okay. Well, you don't have to talk about it. I'm sorry. I really just felt I had to ask you that. How do you feel about that now?' And he said, 'I can't answer that.' I said, 'Are you angry with me for asking?' He said, 'No.' We always smiled at each other after that.

But it was not always within the women's power to keep things friendly. Annie Brotherton recalled that the sweeps of the camp the police often made could be highly threatening: 'It was the times when the police were coming around the base, round all the sites [...] And we got in the tent, the three of us, and [...] I remember them unzipping the tent, and then shining a torch in the tent, and saying, "We're coming in to rape you."' Hannah Schafer also described troubled nights: 'I remember waking up one night, there was a bunch of us sleeping in a big bell tent [...] And I remember waking up and somebody from inside the base was ramming a pole into the tent through the fence. And it was like, you know, about two inches from my head.'

The police, MoD and soldiers were tasked by the base and the local council to make the camp as inhospitable as possible for the women by upturning logs and stones used for seats and pouring water on the campfires. In their interviews, both Lorna Richardson and Judy Harris sang a version of the jazz standard 'Smoke Gets in Your Eyes' with words changed to humorously reflect their experiences:

A policeman said to me,
as he poured water on my tea,
'This land that you can see,
is kept exclusively,
for police and military.'

'Oh, when you joined the force,
was it to run through gorse?
12 men in a van,

with a watering can,
is that how you began?'

The policeman he replied,
as he kicked the logs aside,
'At first I had my doubts,
but they tell so many lies,
smoke gets in your eyes.'

Familiarity did not always breed contempt, however. Sue Say remembered a police officer at the base who dealt with the women regularly on their near-daily actions: 'She was brilliant. She'd always have a laugh, she'd go, "Have you done it?" We'd go, "Yeah," or she'd say, "Did you do this?" and we'd go, "No," and she'd say, "Let them go." Because she knew we'd never deny what we'd actually done [...] she used to release us an awful lot of times because we'd get collared for stuff that we didn't do a lot of the time.'

Becky Griffiths at the time she lived at Greenham, in dialogue with the police. (Paula Allen)

A spirit of neighbourliness even possessed the evictions for a short time when the council sent local Youth Opportunity teenagers along with the bailiffs. Jade laughingly explained:

> The first time they had these the YOpps kids turn up, we had a bit of fun with them. I was following one around saying, 'Perhaps you need to pick that up,' because they were saying, 'Well, what do I do now?' And we'd say, 'Just take that up, and you know, go and put it in the mud sheet, you'll be all right,' and they were going off and doing it – we were telling them what to do! It was really hysterical, because they didn't realise, and the actual bailiffs were getting quite irate about it, because we were treating them like family.

Jade also gave an example of how the women could become experts in subverting situations with the authorities:

> And I remember one time they turned up quite early in the morning and they said, 'Right, well, we'll take your van, are you the driver?' I said, 'Yeah, I'm the driver,' and they said, 'Well you better drive it away now because otherwise we're going to have to impound it.' And I smelled a rat because I thought you don't want to impound it, you probably want to go home and get your tea or something. So I said, 'Do you know what, I've had it with these women here, they just expect me to do everything for them, and they're just taking me for granted – you take the van. Go on, you take it, I think it'll serve them right,' and he was going, 'Oh come on, you can't mean that, they're your friends!' And in the end he was begging me to drive the van away – it was really funny!

The other neighbours who shared the common on and off with the women were Travellers. Ray recalled with amusement the 'local Irish Traveller boys – young men', who would turn up around the fire while the women were spending the evening together, 'And they'd go, "Oh, what do you all do when you get randy, then?" And we'd be like, "Go away, young man!"' This didn't diminish the ardour or optimism of their suitors, however, who would depart with the rejoinder: 'Okay, we're always available if you feel the need!'

5

YOUR DAUGHTERS GREW TO WOMEN, AND YOUR LITTLE BOYS TO MEN

Reflections on motherhood

KATE KERROW

And then your daughters grew to women
And your little boys to men
And you prayed that you were dreaming
When the call came up again
But you proudly smiled and held your tears
As they bravely waved goodbye
And the photos on the mantlepieces
Always made you cry.

From 'Mothers, Daughters, Wives', *The Greenham Songbook*

One of the best-remembered scenes in *Carry Greenham Home* shows Sarah Green giving birth to her son Jay in a bender, with women all around her, passing warm towels as though in a past time, in a past world. The film showed very little of the birth – only a small, striking snapshot of Sarah's labour and, later, a short interview with her holding her baby, looking ruddy and happy.

Sarah's decision to deliver Jay at Greenham wasn't complex. 'That's where I was living,' she said, directly. 'I think it was partly because he was my first child so I didn't know how difficult it was going to be!' Laughing, she added: 'You have this sort of idealistic view that everything's fine. It was probably a naive thing to do.' Although it was May, it had been a very cold night and a challenging experience. 'I was just glad it was over,' she reflected. 'Anyone who's had a baby knows that. I didn't realise it was going to be so difficult [...] My second baby I had in hospital!'

Jay celebrated his second birthday at the camp, spending his first two years in the hub of the women. 'There weren't a lot of children there, but there were children. I did ask him how he felt about it all, and he said he doesn't really remember much about it – just things that are prompted by photographs – but he appreciated being brought up by people who had principles, and fought for something important for everyone, for humanity, for nature. He's a very principled person.'

Lyn Barlow remembered Sarah, Jay and Sarah's partner Arlene:

I liked Sarah and Arlene immensely [...] We used to go to the town cafe for egg and chips. I was really sad when they left [...] I often wonder how that time at Greenham, that backstory, how Jay feels about it now, all these years later. And I remember that there was an undercover reporter at Yellow Gate for a certain amount of time, and we didn't know about it. And she went off and wrote a horrendous article, saying that Jay was basically mistreated – you know, not cared for. And oh god, that ripped through Sarah and Arlene, it really did [...] Typical tabloid.

It was partly the close attention of the press that made Sarah leave Greenham, having concerns for her son's safety:

Mother is carried out, screaming 'You are disgusting'

Baby seized in peace camp court uproar

A THREE-MONTH-OLD baby boy was at the centre of a courtroom tug-of-war yesterday as Greenham 'peace' w o m e n struggled with police.

His mother had carried him into the dock when women from the camp staged a protest at Newbury court in Berkshire in support of a group of defendants.

Magistrates ordered the court to be cleared, and the child was taken from his mother as she was carried outside shouting 'You are disgusting. Give me back my baby.'

Heckled

Former social worker Sarah Green, 38, gave birth to her son, Jay, in a tent at Greenham Common in May.

Yesterday mother and son were watching from the public gallery when six women from the camp outside the Berkshire Cruise missiles base were accused of daubing paint on a U.S. Air Force spy plane, the Blackbird.

Miss Green moved into the dock with some of the defendants while other women lay

Daily Mail Reporter

on the courtroom floor after Ministry solicitor Mr Ian Campbell announced that the charges were being withdrawn.

Magistrates were heckled and jeered, and one of the defendants, former JP Mrs Sarah Hipperson, 55, was dragged from the dock and taken to the cells for refusing to keep quiet. She was later jailed for 14 days for contempt.

About 20 women were then dragged down a flight of stairs from the first-floor courtroom and ejected from the building.

In a din of wailing and shouting, police left Sarah Green and her baby until last, hoping she would walk out voluntarily. But she refused to leave the dock and officers took her baby from her. Cradled by a policewoman,

he was carried downstairs and given back to his mother outside the courthouse.

Another six women—three defendants and three members of the public—were carried to the cells for disrupting proceedings.

It had been alleged that the six women charged cut their way through a fence at the base and daubed paint on the Blackbird and another American warplane at Greenham for last month's international air tattoo.

Miss Isabella Forshall, defending two of the women, said the charges had been 'frivolously brought' and the defendants were entitled to full costs against the prosecution.

The magistrates awarded costs ranging from £18 to £60 to five of the women.

One defendant, 18-year-old Tonia Moon, appeared in the dock dressed as a blackbird, complete with feathers and a yellow beak, and whistled and chirped at intervals throughout the case.

Pictures of happiness

THE wedding day was jinxed—a missed plane to Corfu, a honeymoon hotel crawling with bugs and news that the wedding photographer's camera and film had been stolen. But yesterday, their first wedding anniversary, Mark Paton, 21, and his wife, Clare, 21, were a picture of happiness. Someone had found the stolen camera near their home at Little Stoke, Bristol, a policeman had the film developed and put two and two together—and for the first time they saw their wedding day pictures.

Sarah Green and Jay at the women's camp

Daily Mail, Friday, August 19, 1983

The media were in uproar about Sarah Green and her decision to give birth to and raise a baby at Greenham. (LSE Women's Library)

There was the bad-mother thing. That was one of the things they were throwing at us [...] There were people that had had their children taken from them basically [...] I felt that the military, they were really trying to get at everyone and anyone that they could see had been there for a long time [...] They tried to get at their personal lives in such a way as to divide. So I had to do what I had to do at that point [...] I felt it was unsafe for him [Jay].

The accusations of being a bad mother were plentiful. Fenja Hill was defensive of the decision to raise children at the camp: 'They were very happy. I think one of the reasons we took a lot of pictures of them was because a lot of the media tried to say that all the children were miserable and depressed because it was muddy and wet and horrible. But they weren't.'

It wasn't just the media pressure that concerned the women in regard to the safety of their children. In the mid to late 1980s many women became concerned about the possibility of 'zapping' at the camp; this was the idea that the military were using the women to test the effects of microwave weaponry on the human brain. Sarah shared the women's concerns about zapping: 'I believe that we were targeted with some sort of microwave weaponry. It all went quite crazy at that point [...] I felt it was an unsafe place for my son.'

One of the most significant court cases concerning the impact of Greenham on mothers and children was Elizabeth Beech's trial. Despite her children not living at Greenham, Elizabeth lost custody of them. 'I wanted to live there but I had a six-year-old and four-year-old. My four-year-old was still in playgroup and I thought I couldn't go until he was at school.' At the time, Elizabeth said her husband was very supportive of her going to Greenham, but that their relationship dwindled over time, with him eventually initiating an Emergency Hearing in the magistrates' court. 'I lost custody of my children, with Greenham being cited as the reason – that I'd abandoned them to live at Greenham [...] I went to see a solicitor who said, "Well, nothing will happen because they're bound to have social work reports. They can't just take your children away." But they did.' Elizabeth was granted reasonable access. 'Well, reasonable access didn't take place for two years. I was in and out of court for two years trying to get to see them.'

Some five years later, Elizabeth was living in a squat and she grew friendly with a barrister who lived next door:

He did a bit of investigation, and he said, 'It was really talked about at the time – it was seen as a completely political decision for you to lose custody of those children.' [...] And it was a huge exodus from the camp, women got really scared that they would lose custody of their children due to their presence at Greenham. I mean, it was more effective than zapping or any other methods that might have been used [...] I can remember around that time the camp was in deep trouble with numbers dwindling, including visitor numbers [...] women were really frightened by this judgement [...] me having lost the children [...] It's the big punishment, and it was done.

Elizabeth's sons were supportive of Greenham. One is now an architectural historian, and she believes Greenham affected his career choice. 'He did a great long dissertation on borders and boundaries,' she told us. 'And he set up a conference at Birkbeck University earlier this year for Greenham women and their children.'

Tamsin Clayton's daughter went to Greenham when she was 2 years old, around spring 1982. 'She loved it,' Tamsin said, telling us:

> It was lovely. A lovely place to bring up children actually because there were lots of people that were involved [...] so we always had somebody there. And there were other children [...] so she had people to play with [...] It was just very nice, I think [...] Blue Gate was full of working-class dykes which was where my sort of spiritual home was [...] But it wasn't suitable to have a child there. So we re-established Red Gate [...] Red Gate was there originally, but it wasn't there when I was there [...] It was suitable for children, and then women who wanted to be involved could come for childcare as well.

At the same time, Tamsin acknowledges it could be frightening as a parent. She speaks of the righteous anger at Blue Gate with positivity, but felt she didn't want her child around it: 'I couldn't be there in that environment, I knew I had to create a safer environment.' Additionally, as a mother, Tamsin felt she had to step out of actions that could put her at risk of arrest. Yet, she felt the camp was supportive of different women's needs; women didn't have to be involved if they were likely to be arrested, especially if being arrested would cause personal problems. In these situations, women could stay back and manage the camp.

Tamsin remembers that her daughter wanted to write about Greenham for a project at school. The teacher's response was that it was 'ridiculous', and that it would be almost impossible to find a woman to interview. When Tamsin's daughter responded with, 'Well, my mother was there,' the teacher still vetoed the idea as unsuitable. This story, and ones similar to it, seem to betray the generation of Greenham children who were so active in helping us to develop the archive – men and women who were deeply proud of their mothers' contributions to political history.

Several women discussed their sense of pride at how positively children reflected upon their time at camp, remembering their childhood games at the clearing near Yellow/Main Gate, a Second World War bomb site, or playing with gifts from visitors like the beautiful hand-made dragon kite given to Elizabeth Beech's sons, or living in the ripe world of their imaginations, fuelled by the fascinating ancient woodland around them. They attended school in Newbury from early on in the camp's life, and the women worked together to support mothers who needed to transport children to and from their places of education.

However, some women reported tensions around male children being there, and despite repeated discussions, it was quite some time before the creation of a cut-off age for boys became the agreed solution. Vicki Smith also echoed the tensions: 'There was a bit of discussion about when we should ask them to go back to their fathers – I think we decided on age 10. There were certainly no adolescent males there.' Elizabeth Greenland remembered the women at Yellow Gate hearing a rumour that there was a man at the camp. Laughing, she told us: 'It was just my son – he was only seven!'

Most of the women we interviewed were positive about children being at the camp, but some felt it wasn't the right environment. Vicki, now a child psychologist, said she had reservations about whether they should have been there:

Looking back, I think it was probably inappropriate to have them around. They weren't at school and narrow education is impoverishing for a child. I think that, broadly speaking, children should be with other children of their own age, and with a range of different people. It was a very narrow political slice there. Broadly speaking, we all had the same kind of views [...] There was a lot of swearing, there were a lot of open conversations – very open conversations that perhaps very young children could have been protected from for a few more years. But, you know, organisation-wise, they weren't a bother. Everybody helped to care for them, so it was no problem for a mum to have kids there, because whichever tent they went into, or whatever car they went into, they were safe. You know, they had twelve mothers instead of just one.

Women living at Greenham and visitors to the camp tied items of emotional significance, often photographs of family members, to the fence. These were symbols of what they loved, and stood to lose, in a nuclear holocaust. (Bridget Boudewijn)

Elizabeth Greenland felt that the children benefitted greatly from having a Greenham mother:

> None of the people I know came away from it with anything other than being really proud of their mothers, or being really proud of themselves [...] Women banded together to look after the children – it was definitely organised in such a way. The children weren't damaged in any way by it. If anything, it was a great thing that they were involved. Certainly, that age group of children now, if they discover that their mother was also involved at Greenham Common, they immediately have a bond with each other.
>
> My son was very conscious that at the time he was probably was the only man on site apart from the policemen. He thought that was funny. The policemen thought it was funny too – in fact he used to be good friends with some of them. They used to take him off and buy him hotdogs. He used to get on well with them, and they were all a nice bunch of chaps.
>
> I remember it was very cold, and so we'd just go and stay for a week or something, and then we'd go back home and wash and everything, and then we'd go back again [...] I mean, camping in the snow, the children thought that was really good fun and it wasn't cold once we'd got all the blankets put on the floor, and the sleeping bags in.
>
> It was definitely an experience I'm really, really pleased they experienced with me. I was very much a mother that treated my children like friends, so if I was doing something like that, I would have wanted them to be with me, and I think it was definitely a good thing for them to have been involved in.

Rebecca Mordan, who visited the camp when she was about 5 years old, warmly remembered the regular visits to camp with her mother as informative and compelling. In the early 1980s, Marie Knowles played a significant organisational role in Camberley CND, and had been using her position to facilitate support for the camp. Rebecca remembers being at CND workshops with Marie where Greenham women were asked to come and teach the principles of NVDA for use in CND demonstrations. 'I would be kicking around, watching, waiting, listening,' she said, explaining:

> They created an improvisation about what to do when being charged by police-horses, and what to do with their bodies, how you would go all heavy. Also processes like having a witness and protecting the people around you. I remember they cried and hugged each other after the improvisation. I was fascinated. I can see now them playing out the different parts. Talking about it, it sounds like it might look silly, but I remember feeling that is exactly what it would be like. They were always so lovely to me, listened to my little emotions, valued my voice.

Rebecca also remembers going with her mother and other Greenham women to help drop campaign flyers in their local town:

> I remember thinking I don't want all my pets to die! I was very passionate little girl about all this stuff. I also had that child-logic of believing that if you explain something to someone they will understand and it will be fine. I remember one guy being really furious with me one day, and holding me to account, making me basically tell him why nuclear armament was such a bad idea. And I felt like I had to bring all my powers together, like this was the moment it had all been leading to [...] and then all of these women just swooped in to support me! They were all, 'Quite right Rebecca, and another thing, and another thing!' and to him they were all, 'Shame on you for being like that with a little girl!'
>
> It was a very interesting early experience of motherhood – in one way, I had this intense relationship with my mum, but in another, I was in a village of women. At Greenham, I felt like I could go up to anybody, I felt so safe. I remember hanging with the women, saluting the women, just being so fascinated by the world of grown-ups. I remember Embrace the Base which was massive. There were tons of families. The sound of so many women singing. Holding hands with my mum on one side and another woman on the other. I remember just looking up at them in awe. They were swaying the fence down,

swaying with the singing, and my mum was beaming down at me, elated. I remember thinking, 'My mum is so cool and these women are so cool.'

But it was clear that motherhood also presented difficulties for mothers who wanted to be active at Greenham. All of the mothers we spoke to told us they'd thought very deeply about what was the right thing for their children to be doing, alongside trying to find balance and carve out an identity for themselves.

Lynne Wilkes had just had a baby in 1981. Of Greenham, she said: 'I felt my heart was there, but my physical presence felt – well, my intuition – said, "no, it's really important to be safe with this baby" [...] But it was all beginning then and we were living in London – in Brixton, at the time of the riots.' After completing a teacher training degree at Goldsmith's University, she lived in Reading for a time, bonding with some like-minded women at the Reading Women's Centre. 'I split up from my husband in that time, when Joe was three. When you're going through that phase, you're looking for sisterhood and support from women, and women in similar situations, and women in general, I think. So it was really an easy sort of route to begin. I didn't have to even try. It was like falling on my lap, and it felt right then.' Lynne became very involved with Night Watch. 'I think it was great to support, because of having such a tiny child. I was breastfeeding him until he was three. So I was very much involved in that, and bringing him up was my priority. But each time I could go to Greenham, I would.'

Many of the women we interviewed were supporters and visitors of Greenham, as well as women who were residents at the camp. While the women who visited often downplayed the importance of their role, offering respect to the women who lived full time at the camp, the women who were residents talked of how crucial the women who came to support them were – how they were a key part of keeping Greenham going, providing the women with much-needed company, food and general assistance, as well as completing actions. They believed visiting women were just as much Greenham women as those who lived there. Night Watch was mostly run by camp supporters, and was a crucial service to the residents. Many supporters were mothers who didn't feel able to live full time at camp due to having children. 'I don't know what the right word is, but we were just there to support and protect them – like guardians,' Lynne said. 'To allow them the safety of sleep, and energy for what they were choosing. You know, they were putting their lives into Greenham Common every day [...] The more I went there, the more I got more intrigued. When I was no longer breastfeeding, I felt I could sort of do a little bit more, you know, and that felt right.'

Lynne had Joe when she was 24:

Greenham was an awakening [...] I think if I hadn't have had Joe, I would have been there in a very different capacity. You know, I might have been living there. I might have been doing all sorts, but having a child sets you on a different path [...] I feel very blessed that I could explore this side of things [...] Being a single parent, having a lot of women friends, it felt a really good space [...] When you do have a child, your whole fear thing goes into another level, you know, before that, fear seems so different. And now you're going – actually, this isn't just about me [...] I had little person that I was responsible for. So that was always my priority, had to keep getting back for that [...] Most of us had to get back for our kids to take them to nursery and school [...] If you're being chucked out by the army and the police, they could chuck you out anywhere, and it's a very wide perimeter. But for the grace of god, I just knew I had to get back to take Joe to nursery!

Later, the art of healing became a passion of Lynne's and influenced her parenting. 'I started to see the male and female energies in a different way, because it's very easy to be at Greenham and to have that sort of "Men are bastards, men are trash" thing [...] I thought I've got to be careful because I've got a little boy, and I can't keep saying that because he's going to be a little man one day, but it was a phase you have to go through to come out and see the wider solutions.' While she wasn't quiet, Lynne remembers choosing her words carefully as a parent: 'I was like, "my god, they said that!" [...] I wasn't afraid to talk but I didn't use language which I probably would have liked to have used.' Yet she still found ways to demonstrate an identity which embraced motherhood and her Greenham spirit:

I got a number two – I was looking like Sinead O'Connor. And then my little boy got the same hair cut – we both had a tiny plait made from the remains of the long hair. That felt great to do, that sense of being very comfortable with my face. I didn't need my hair to hide my face. I actually quite liked my face and I felt strong, you know, and as a single parent, you're looking for a sense of inner strength.

Lynne says she's never spoken to her son about his experience of Greenham, about his recollections. At the time of our interview, Joe had just had a baby, and Lynne had become a grandmother. 'He was quite young – I mean, kids of that age just go with the flow, don't they? He loved poking fires – there's a picture of him doing that. He was just always poking the fire, had a fascination with fires.'

Lynne went to Greenham as a mother, but she also experienced a formative relationship with a woman in which she felt like a daughter: 'I got very close with this German woman who was a similar age to my mum [...] She never had a daughter and my mum was in Africa and it felt like we had this lovely sort of symbiotic relationship.'

Judy Harris remembered another way in which the role of the mother arose at camp: 'There was this woman, Mabel who, oh god, she was amazing,' she told us:

She must have been well into her eighties because I remember her son didn't like her coming because he felt that it wasn't safe and stuff. And we were all a bit worried about her. But she used to come up every couple of months and stay over. And I can remember her being at the fence, talking to these soldiers and just telling them off. It was like she was like your Nanna, you know, they couldn't say anything to her! They would be a bit shamefaced when she was saying, 'You shouldn't be doing this.'

Anyone who comes to research the women's peace camp will likely find that sources written from an outside perspective tend to identify the women as mothers foremost. Certainly, a simplistic reading of the campaign would be to assert that the women were at Greenham primarily to save children and future generations of children, appealing to maternalistic ideals and the idea of women as biologically destined to be better nurturers and peacemakers: the patriarchal stereotypes of womanhood. It is true that some slogans and campaign material appealed to 'the Mother', including the very first pamphlet designed to rally support by Women for Life on Earth. It's also true, across the broad spectrum of the thousands of women who attended Greenham across its history, that many were mothers who, as well as devoting their lives to nurturing their own children, campaigned through compassion for the world's children. Mary Birch remembers the sense of motherhood as central to her on the day of Embrace the Base: 'Some people brought their children, and a lot of people brought photographs of their children, or babies' garments and we hung all these things on the fence, so if anybody came along they could see it there – so babies clothes and children's school clothes. All sorts of childish toys and things, because it was essentially saying, "Save our children".'

However, the sheer number of women who visited Greenham across its history naturally meant that there were a host of varied reasons for their attendance. Obviously, one of the women's key motives was to explore the role of women in peacemaking and political campaigning, and to find new ways to work towards peace and against violence. The thousands of women who attended Greenham were diverse – from the young, free and single radical lesbians at Blue Gate, to women who had witnessed global conflict first hand. One slogan read: 'We've lived through two World Wars, we're here, determined there'll never be a third!' And, of course, women wanted to challenge the stereotypes associated with themselves as care-givers. In one sketch, a mother pushing a pram proclaims: 'I want a future for my child!' and next to her a woman dressed in the characteristic Greenham garb responds: 'I wouldn't mind a future for myself.'[15] Mica May told us:

People would come and women, especially women with kids, would shake my hand and say, 'Thank you for doing this for us', which was lovely, but I said to them, 'I'm not doing it for you, I'm doing it … well, I'm just doing it.' And it wasn't for anybody else [...] you know, women can only be two kinds of person, and one is that you've got to be bleeding and damaged and always doing it for somebody else, and I didn't want to be connected to that stereotype. I'm happy enough to be a nurturer, but I was not going to be the sacrificer of myself.

Vicki Smith echoed the idea that a great variety of women from different generations with different agendas came to support the campaign:

For a lot of women, this was brand new for them – they'd been married, they'd had their kids in the seventies when a lot of women were up and moving and getting politically aware, and they'd suddenly found themselves in their fifties with no kind of life of their own, and they thought this is something that I can belong to [...] Everybody was welcome. Any sexual orientation, absolutely any age [...] The ideas women were bringing and sharing around the campfire were extraordinary [...] four generations of women together sharing ideas about our political possibilities and freedoms and rights.

Writer and campaigner Nina Millns, in her thirties at the time of our interview, went to a London nursery school which had been set up by a group of Greenham women in the early 1980s. She remembered the experience very clearly, and the staff as a group of very strong, warm women from a variety of backgrounds:

Most of them were white. We did have some Canadians. We had some South Africans, and we had a few workers who were Black or Asian or mixed. My understanding was that there wasn't a hierarchy, they were all equal and they made decisions collectively. They had meetings every week to collectively make the decisions about the way the nursery was being run [...] The second thing I remember is that they wanted us to address them as workers. So if we had a problem, or if we needed help, we'd raise our hands and call for a worker, so we wouldn't say Miss Brown, or teacher or whatever, we'd say, 'Worker, worker', and someone would come [...] It was an acknowledgement that that's what they were there to do, and that they were all equal, you know with that title.

Nina emphasised the strength of the women around her. 'They were just such strong personalities. I remember there was one woman called Mary Susan who was a clown from Canada [...] She was just larger than life. She had this laugh – she'd sit on the stairs and just laugh for a good five minutes, and it was so infectious [...] But each one of the women was very, very different.'

Nina remembered that the children's books were chosen very carefully:

> My favourite book I was given – I remember the lead character was a little Black girl in a wheelchair. And she got to go on lots of adventures, and she was the hero of the stories. And that was just a normal thing for me [...] That was my first experience of books, and learning who was allowed to go on what adventures, and who was allowed to be the protagonist in their own adventures, and what they were capable of, what they were allowed to do and who was allowed to be at the centre of the story.

Nursery rhymes too were tweaked and changed to create balance. Nina remembered a version of 'Baa Baa Black Sheep': 'Baa Baa Black Sheep have you any wool? Yes, woman, yes woman, three bags full. One for the mistress, one for the dame, and one for the little girl who lives down the lane.'

Many of the workers were openly gay, queer, bisexual. 'We met their girlfriends, their partners,' Nina said, explaining:

> It was a community, so a lot of what was happening went beyond just the nursery hours, you know. I remember lots of parties [...] I remember boys walking around in dresses from the fancy dress box [...] I remember us being encouraged to just explore our identity with as little conditioning as possible in terms of gender normative messages. I don't remember the words 'girls and boys' ever being used. I might be wrong. But I do feel that very possibly they would have made a decision not to even make distinctions of that sort.

Additionally, Nina remembered there being a structure to the day that prioritised free play with plenty of creativity:

An image created by taking a picture of the child on the beach and superimposing it in the enlarger with the dandelion clock, creating a monoprint. (Bridget Boudewijn)

We had a little garden where we could go out and get messy, and you know, lots of paint and artwork, and lots of cooking and shopping, for both the boys and the girls. But what I remember is that every day ended with us in one room, sitting together, singing songs, talking about things, telling stories. I don't specifically remember us being asked for our opinion, but what I do feel is that we were encouraged to feel like a community that was equal. I certainly felt listened to, included, encouraged in every way. I felt very, very free and when I looked around, I just saw kids that were just free to absolutely be themselves, with as little of that kind of external conditioning as possible.

The nursery Nina talks of is a clear example of the 'Greenham Women Everywhere' motto. The women went into Greenham to champion new ways of living, working and campaigning for a more progressive world. The lifestyles being lived at Greenham were channelled into new social projects that ran alongside the camp, and the nursery Nina attended shows the ways in which dismantling patriarchal structures can start with children.

Ann Pettitt.

Sue Lent.

Maria Ragusa.

Judith Baron.

Alison Napier.

Jill 'Ray' Raymond.

Jade Britton.

Sarah Green.

Elizabeth Beech.

Helen MacRae.

Hannah Schafer.

Peggy Seeger.

Frankie Armstrong.

Mica May.

Illona Linthwaite.

Janet Smith.

Josetta Malcolm.

Lyn Barlow.

Sue Say.

Sally Hay.

Elizabeth Woodcraft.

Becky Griffiths – now a purveyor of delicious Mother's Ruin gin!

Carolyn Francis.

Maggie Parks.

(All photographs taken by Christine Bradshaw at the time of the interviews)

6

QUEERS AND HAGS

The media

REBECCA MORDAN

Here at Greenham on a spree,
Financed by the KGB,
Dirty women squatters in the mud,
Mostly vegetarian when we're not devouring men,
Foreigners and other forms of scud.[16]

Mr. Breshnev makes sure we're kept in vodka,
With sealed copies of Karl Marx in plastic bags,
Our children here live miserably with rats and deprivation,
But what can you expect from queers and hags?

From 'Here at Greenham on a Spree', by Gillian Booth

From the beginning it was clear that the relationship between the camp and the media was going to be, at the very least, strained. An iconic photograph or article could see the camp shoot to public attention, or could just as easily see a young woman outed and then ostracised from her family. The women wanted to get their myriad of messages out to the wider world, but they wanted to do so collectively and not through a male filter; most professional journalists and photographers, who were generally men, wanted to pop in, get a soundbite from a spokesperson and grab a sensational image to sell their angle of the story. And that was if the attention of the press could be won at all.

Starting out as quite paternalistic, some local press and national big hitters like *The Guardian* first commended Greenham's bravely maternal attributes, applauding the efforts of the mothers of Women for Life on Earth to defend the future for their children. Then, like the confused father of rebellious teens, they drew back as the women stepped out of the traditional bounds of motherhood – leaving husbands at home, creating their women-only space, becoming increasingly direct and disobediant in their actions – and only stepped in to report periodically across the near two decades of the camp's life. And into the gaps flooded a very different media attention, much more like that of an abusive partner. Led by papers like the *Sun* and the *Daily Mail*, this media focus set about to discredit, demoralise and, in some cases, destroy the women and their camp. But as their exposure to the press grew, the women became increasingly savvy and were able to turn the tables and redefine the narrative, certainly influencing and arguably changing the discourse about nuclear weapons both at home and abroad.

'This is basically how we were portrayed in the press: we were a load of filthy lesbians bringing our kids up in squalor. And we were being financed by the Russians,' Hazel Pegg told us when we asked the women how they were represented in the media. Our interviewees identified several themes that came up time and again. 'One was definitely "filthy lesbians",' Becky Griffiths said. 'The other was kind of [...] there was a whole thing about we'd been infiltrated by Russians, and it was all kind of like communist plot. And then there was a whole other thing that we were just silly. Our thinking was woolly, we didn't have any proper political kind of analysis, and we were just kind of

The Greenham women often humorously inverted media and government messages. (Bridget Boudewijn)

over-emotional. Bordering on the whole hysteria thing, you know, women are hysterical creatures.'

Alison Napier agreed:

I think it was very easy to ridicule Greenham at the time. I've always been interested in what the press does, and the press was shameful [...] I remember one tabloid had a dramatic headline which went something like, 'Woolly-headed, woolly-hatted, lentil-eating lesbians', and I quite liked the alliteration in that, I thought that was quite a good headline. In terms of the truth, it wasn't technically wrong, I guess, maybe the 'woolly-headed' was a bit unfortunate, but everything else in it was true [...] But there was no discussion about the issues [...] this was the 1980s, and we were in Mrs Thatcher's time. The mines were being shut down, and poll tax had come into Scotland to see if we liked it, which of course we didn't. And it was a very oppressive, anti-humanity time. It was a very cruel time.

Sarah Green echoed this perspective: 'I think – well the one I remember was the "woolly-headed women". We were looked at as if we were stupid. And that we didn't know what we were doing. But [...] eighty per cent of people were against cruise missiles, especially American cruise missiles on British soil. It was difficult to undermine us totally.'

Like Alison, Sue Say noticed that the press picked up on some things that might not be technically untrue, but would amplify them at the expense of all other facts, using them to obscure reality and the women's messages. According to the tabloids: 'Some women were "dirty, scruffy, lesbian, pot-smoking, hippie junkies", you know? No, they weren't. But this was the image that was portrayed.' However, she went on: 'Were they lesbian? Yes.' But again this wasn't the whole story, because as Sue remembered at Yellow Gate:

There were lots of straight women, there were lots of different women, but people went to type – so they were all women, therefore they've all got to be lesbians [...] I would say probably half to three quarters were lesbian. But I wouldn't say more than that. You know, I was thinking back to some of the some of the friends that I had there, at Yellow Gate

– about eleven or twelve straight women I can think of straight away. The lesbians – probably twenty of them, that I can think of straight away – so 'they're all lesbians' was a bit over the top.

The media sensationalism over the sexuality of the women was at odds with the day-to-day reality of the camp, where, as Penny Gulliver notes: 'Obviously a lot of stuff around sexual politics was talked about and you know, we were predominately lesbian [...] but it wasn't a big deal.' This environment where lesbians were not only safe and accepted, but the norm, actually outnumbering the heterosexual women at many gates, was in complete opposition to the wider world. 'I'd sort of just realised I was a lesbian not long before I discovered Greenham,' Hannah Schafer explained. 'So camp was great for me because where I lived was quite homophobic [...] one guy who accused me of having an affair with his girlfriend [...] like he nearly kicked me head in [...] So it was great for me to go to Greenham and just see "lesbian" written on the tents. Like it was a badge of pride, not something to sort of keep your head down about, you know what I mean?'

Becky Griffiths also spoke about the vital role Greenham played for lesbians, especially for young women like the 17-year-old she was when she moved to Yellow Gate. 'I was coming out as a lesbian, and arriving somewhere where there were women, where they were gay women – the first gay women I'd ever seen! Because I'd lived somewhere where nobody was gay, except for perhaps me – and how terrifying is that?'

Both Hannah and Penny remembered during their time at Blue Gate a tabloid journalist who drove her car into a ditch just near them. 'I don't know if she did it on purpose or not,' Hannah recalled, 'but [...] she drove her car into the ditch, and then was all upset about it. So women were being supportive [...] and pulled the car out.' Penny agreed:

We went over [...] and not only did we get her out, carry her practically to the fire, and sit her down, give her a cup of tea, see if she was all right, but we got her Mini out of the ditch because there was no way else it was going to get out. And the next week in the paper: 'Molested by lesbians at Blue Gate – their hands were all over me!' blah blah blah, and we were all like, 'The woman had crashed her car!'

Janet Smith, who was working away from Blue in a laboratory at the time the story came out, saw the article through the eyes of both friends and colleagues:

> I knew the women who'd helped her and she'd written the article about [...] what they said had happened was she'd driven a car into the ditch and they'd pulled it out, and her car wasn't usable. So they'd found her a place in a bender to sleep for the night. And then she wrote this article about being scared for her life because there was a lesbian in the next tent – and it was just really nasty, and stupid [...] and of course all the technicians in my lab had read this article [...] I told them what rubbish it was.

Targeting the women for abuse was not limited to those living full time at camp. Helen MacRae supported and visited Greenham from the Kentish Town Women's Centre, and one day, while a group of around fifty women were there planning an action, as 'Declan and his mates' were running the creche, 'this woman came in, very well dressed, a very beautiful woman'. Helen remembered that 'she looked wealthy. And lovely blonde hair. I remember her leather jacket and she asked if she could join, and we welcomed her warmly. Well, she was a journalist – we didn't know that – she was from the *Daily Express*. And she wrote the most revolting article, and there was a big cartoon as well about this burly, lesbian, boiler-suited woman. She distorted everything. The article was full of lies and blatant distortions.'

Not prepared to take this misrepresentation lying down, Helen wrote to the *Express*, challenging the editor: '"Bet you don't publish this" [...] I wanted him to see that this woman had been welcomed, and had then trivialised something that was almost sacred. Because none of them were doing anything to raise consciousness about this. So she'd mocked something that was kind of pure.'

Wilful distortion and malignment from the press saw Fenja Hill being pursued not just by tabloids but by TV networks also. The story they were all desperate to get her comment on was that she and her MoD officer husband had moved to the base, where she had met a Greenham woman through the fence, and then left her family to live with her lover on the other side at the camp. Fenja told our interviewer a far less sensational and more emotionally complex version of what actually happened. She was from a military family herself and had married at only 20; her husband then applied to become an MoD officer so 'we moved to Newbury and he was based at Greenham'. She told her interviewer: 'Everywhere that I lived as a child, the only thing I ever saw was nuclear families [...] it never occurred to me that there were other alternatives and other options [...] I just followed the pattern that I thought I was supposed to follow.' By the time Fenja moved to Greenham, she was becoming close to her cousin Tamsin Clayton because 'she was at camp and I was really unhappy, so I used to go and visit her camp'. It was this relationship that saw Fenja start to spend time beyond the fence:

> I didn't first go there for the politics. In fact, I was beyond apolitical because I think I'd just been living in a bubble all my life. I mean, I was twenty-eight when I was first at camp, and I hadn't ever really been interested. I remember as a child if the news came on, we all went, 'Oh, god, news', and buggered off somewhere else. I went to camp, and I started to meet women, and get involved, and I was already on the brink of separating from my husband. And it was difficult because the local media – well it wasn't even local, it was national – I don't even know how they got hold of it – but somehow they got hold of the idea that there was a woman who was married to someone who was working on the base, who was living at camp, and I wasn't even living there at that point – I was visiting, as Tamsin used to come with her daughter.

We also spoke to Tamsin, who recalled Fenja visiting her and bringing her children, which her husband 'didn't like it much at all. But I mean, realistically, their marriage was already over.' Tamsin described:

> And it was through Greenham, that she found out that she could get benefits, that she didn't actually have to stay in a marriage that she was dreadfully unhappy in. She didn't realise that [...] she'd sort of stayed in a marriage that she wasn't happy in for a long time, because she didn't realise that she could escape. So she then went on and

The British government's 'Protect & Survive' booklet advises use of brown paper bags in the event of nuclear war. Photo by Raissa Page (deceased), 1982. (Jenny Engledow)

escaped. So I imagine we sort of wanted somewhere for the kids to play safely. And so we said, 'Oh, let's go and reopen Red Gate.' And that's what we did.

This process of liberation and self-discovery, supported by family and friends, was a far cry from the lurid tale of wantonness and child abandonment on which Fenja found herself hounded by journalists to give comment.

From the obsessive frenzy in the media about the women's sexuality, it is easy to see that the camp posed a threat to the establishment through the alternative way the women modelled sex and relationships. As women left their houses to live on the common, often bringing up children collectively, or in some cases leaving them with their fathers, the camp was seen to be challenging the heterosexual societal norm of the nuclear family, in which men went out to work and women stayed at home to take care of the children. This threat led to easy low blows from the press being regularly levelled at them, focusing on them as examples of deviant womanhood and unfit mothers.

Sarah Green and her then partner Arlene were living at Yellow Gate when she gave birth to her son Jay, and the family lived there until he was two and a half years old. Sarah remembers that the press attention 'changed after Embrace the Base, because that level of support, that level of women saying the same thing at the same time, I don't think that's ever happened before or since – thirty thousand women holding hands. That's powerful.' The scale of this action showed a conservative press the potential the camp had to radicalise a large portion of the female population, and it was outraged. Sarah remembered the lengths the press started to go to in order to undermine the camp:

There was certainly people that came around pretending they were ordinary people, and they were actually the press. And then they would be writing all sorts of things in the press later. And I mean, I had that happen to me quite a few times – 'that Sarah Green said this!' – and they always made me look like an idiot. But I was talking to just someone from the street, and I wasn't really answering the questions, because I didn't know who they were.

Lyn Barlow recounted to us the sense of hurt and betrayal she and other women experienced when a visitor they thought they had bonded with over the course of a few days or weeks turned out to have been a tabloid reporter determined to represent the camp as negatively as possible. 'We were all lesbian,' she recalled, 'or we were all aggressive, confrontational. And yeah, we were all of those things, but much more besides, you know what I mean – but that was what they wanted to see and portray.'

Hazel described 'this double page spread in the *Mail*' about a fellow Yellow-Gater, Elizabeth Beech, whose husband took her to court for custody of their children and won:

> It's kind of like this is the system saying, 'Do not step out of line or we'll take your children.' You know, 'Bolshie women who step out too far, this is what will happen, your children will be gone, you will be vilified in public at length.' Yeah, that was the system, flashing out this great big red flag warning to women, 'Don't step too far out of line, because this is what they can do to you.'

Her friend Gillian Booth added: 'And it worked! A lot of women stopped coming to Greenham Common, women who had children. It worked.' Negative coverage and press infiltration took their toll on the women at camp.

The drip-feed of hyper-negativity in the press certainly had an effect on the perception the public had of the Greenham women. 'I can remember the first time I went to Greenham, you know, I was so prejudiced, I was so naive,' remembered local CND member Annei Soanes. 'I thought, oh my god, what's it going to be like? Because I might meet *lesbians*. What was I going to do if I met a lesbian?' Her fellow interviewee Margaret McNeill agreed, elaborating: 'There was this huge amount of misinformation [...] all of the women could be discredited because we were lesbians, we'd left our families to fend for themselves, etc., etc. So therefore, we were the dregs of humanity.' Both women remember the reaction of those around them being influenced by this misinformation. Margaret remembered being 'at an evening class once and I said I was rather tired because I'd spent the previous night at Greenham'. Shocked, the woman she was speaking to said, 'Oh, my goodness, are they all lesbians?' Before she could answer, Margaret recalls the teacher stepping in to her rescue by asking: 'How the hell should she know?'

Annei also talked to us about having to stand up against the misconceptions and prejudices about the camp when discussing it with acquaintances:

I remember one of my mother's friends actually, when he was ridiculing me about what I was doing, he said, 'And you know what, those women?', he said, 'they've ruined Greenham.' I said, 'What do you mean?' He said, 'The wildlife.' 'Do you know,' he said, 'there's no wildlife around Greenham now, nothing. Why? Because of the women.' And the huge American air base! But that's an example of how people made judgements based on nothing. You know, there were lots of fantasies around it. And these women, what were they doing? Why weren't they at work? Or why weren't they looking after their children? Why weren't they at home looking after their families? Because that's what women do. You know, these women were breaking the rules – they were being oppositional to what was judged decent.

Margaret agreed. 'Yes, definitely. I think we were interfering with men's work. This is what men do. What do women know about warfare and security? So the fact that we'd risen up against – and, I guess they might have taken it personally.' She then added, laughing: 'I hope so! [...] Because there were some boring old farts out there. One of my husband's relations – he was a civil servant, and he used to take me to one side and warn me that we were being infiltrated – women were being infiltrated by undesirables. Really? "Really! How awful." Whereas to my mind, the undesirables who'd infiltrated us were the Americans with their sodding bombs!'

We asked who people thought the Greenham camp might be infiltrated by and Margaret explained: 'Oh, well, foreigners obviously [...] people who wanted the wherewithal to steal the plutonium, or uranium [...] terrorists basically who are going to be amongst us, so that when we broke in, they could then break in and steal a bomb or something [...] it was absolutely hilarious.'

The negative stereotypes that the press conjured and encouraged soon affected the Greenham women's closest relationships. Penny Gulliver remembered a Scottish woman from a small village who was targeted by a Scottish newspaper which took stories and pictures of her back to her home. 'She wasn't allowed basically back into the village, never mind her own home.'

Annie Brotherton summed the situation up when we asked if any of her family visited her at Greenham. She explained: 'They did in the early eighties, but that stopped [...] by '83.' This was when evictions were at their height and, with their image vilified in the press, the women were experiencing renewed aggression from locals:

> Hostile, you know, the cars that were driving past, 'Fucking lesbians, fucking' [...] like they didn't know that there was cruise missiles right there – or their house was looking out over what was their common land that's now cruise missiles aimed at Russia – they didn't mind that. What they minded was look down and there's dirty, hairy lesbians – that's what they most wanted, you know, to get rid of lesbians – I know, it's bizarre.

Lyn Barlow broke into the base most days, increasingly focusing on stealing documents and taking photographs to prove how government press releases about the base, its practices and security often did not match secret government policy and correspondence. She soon found that most journalists wouldn't touch this information, and developed a high regard for those who broke the mould, like Janie Hulme and Duncan Campbell:

> Janie who worked for the *Morning Star*, she was brilliant. She was the first we'd go to [...] built up quite a relationship with Janie, because she would be probably the only journalist who would actually go on and print regardless of being told not to. I mean, one document we got out, we took it around the press, and no one would touch it. It was like a hot potato. Whether there'd been a D-notice put on it, we don't know. But Janie Hulme would run it. And that's how I first got contact with Duncan, because Duncan would run it. But the rest of

the papers, even left wing papers like the *Guardian*, you know, we still had that prickly relationship.

Despite having this 'prickly relationship' thrust upon them, the women kept their camp alive and, in the case of women like Mica May, even managed to keep their sense of humour:

I had a little badge that said 'Witch' on it, and I don't remember what his name was – the Tory politician from Newbury came up to speak to us – and I spoke to him, I can't remember what it was I said, but I do remember it appearing in the paper the following week, that [...] he was spoken to by one of the witches, and he's never been ill before, but he lost his voice as a result! And I do remember thinking, 'You're an idiot, just shut up,' so maybe I did make him lose his voice!

As the women learned to live under the lens of the media, they also learned through analysing and experiencing it how to use it better to their advantage. Becky Griffiths told us: 'It was a revelation to me that you could be at an action, see what had happened, say clearly what had happened to a reporter, and then read about it in the paper the next day, and it be a completely different thing.' Jade Britton had the same disillusionment with the press, but also found it liberating as it gave the narrative of the camp back to the women. 'It shows you that actually Greenham didn't need the press [...] because what the press said wasn't necessarily true, but you can talk to other people, and even talking to one other person can change somebody's view. And, you know, if you do that, all of a sudden you're a movement.' Becky described the subtleties of conflicting narratives and how her perception of reporting changed after speaking to the press, that it 'taught me a lot about reading newspapers even today [...] the police description of an action was so different from ours. And yet, somehow, the facts were sort of the same. The facts were the same, but it was how they were reported, and what people said about them. And that was kind of an eye-opener to me.'

'I remember reading court reports of places that I'd been to, you know, places when I'd been there, and just sort of thinking well, the press never actually tell the truth,' said Janet Smith. 'So that was something else I got from Greenham, I guess I learned some media savviness. I learned that the press will write what they want to write, and if the truth's not quite what they want, they'll change it.'

Lessons like these soon taught the women the importance of having your press contact at actions if possible, giving your side of the story, or at least ensuring a story of some kind appeared. Sue Bolton and Bridget Boudewijn attended several large actions at Greenham together, and were inspired to campaign against the moving of nuclear weapons and nuclear waste around their home of the Isle of Wight. 'Whenever we did an action it was always either photographed or it was on other news,' Bridget explained to us, remembering how hard Sue worked to get press along:

> Because I think she knew very much that it's no use just doing it and saying, 'Oh, we've done that.' People need to know about it. And we did become known as Ventnor Peace Women, lots of people thought we were a bit bonkers. And some people thought we were right [...] But we put it out there and it was quite often in the newspapers – often on the front of the newspapers, what was happening.

Sue also took part in an international publicity stunt that shows how inventive the women became at courting press attention to promote their messages. 'We found this law back from about 1400 and something that said, the Americans couldn't put weapons or war on somebody else's land. It was something like that,' Sue told us, recalling that she was invited by the American legal team to join them in New York to testify at the trial 'to take the president to court'. Ronald Reagan didn't actually turn up, but Sue remembers being 'outside the courthouse in the middle of the square in New York, and the main media from all around the world are interviewing us'.

When the women started coming to trial themselves in British courts, they were defended by a young Elizabeth Woodcraft, who was then working in 'radical chambers, whose aim in life was to, you know, fight

This banner subverts the government-sponsored anti-littering campaign, capitalising on the public's recognition of the Keep Britain Tidy slogan to make an anti-nuclear point. (Bridget Boudewijn)

for truth and justice and human rights and so on'. She was profoundly impressed by the women who, unlike other clients, insisted on building their own defence with her. This way the women could use their own cases as platforms to expose the international human rights abuses inherent in the making of nuclear weapons in the press. She explained: 'They were incredible [...] and there was clever stuff, you know, I mean, talking about bomb-making and uranium mining.'

Elizabeth also noted, 'as time went on', that the profile of the women did start to change, 'particularly in the *Guardian*, and things like that'. She felt that 'people began to react very badly to seeing women, you know, shoved into prison day after day, it reminded people of the Suffragettes and everyone knew how bad that had been [...] they had to sort of take it more seriously and think about it'.

The collective, lateral nature of the peace camp presented its own problems and opportunities in regard to the press. 'It was nebulous, or it wasn't an organisation, there wasn't a leader, there wasn't a website [...] so the press didn't know who to speak to,' observed Alison Napier:

> If they wanted to speak to somebody they would turn up at the gate and whoever was there would speak to them, and it might be a radical-lesbian-anarchist-pacifist-separatist, or it might be somebody who was wanting to stand for the Labour Party in the next council elections. It could be anybody, so they had such a wide range of, I guess, soundbites coming at them – the press.

Blue Gate embraced the possibility this offered for women to share the limelight and gain experience of giving interviews by coming up with a system where nobody was interviewed on their own. 'You always worked with at least two people doing that interview,' Ray told us. This ensured that quieter or less confident women were supported and not overshadowed and that statements could be issued from different perspectives of class or race in the same interview.

This system helped the women at Blue Gate to counter what they had learned about the less trustworthy side of press attention. Ray explained: 'We had to be very careful with the press [...] because you know they'll misquote you, and they won't put the bits in that you think are important. Nobody wanted to talk to the press, and we didn't do it on our own. We'd always say: "All the stars are in the sky, we don't have leaders here."'

Hazel Pegg described how they tried to 'stop hierarchy' but how complicated that could become in practice. 'Yeah, it wasn't entirely successful, where you had people like Helen John and Rebecca Johnson and a couple of others who floated to the top,' she explained. 'And it's very difficult because the press like to have a name and a face [...] We tried to fight against hierarchies like that and say we have no leaders and no spokeswoman [...] But still, some people were better at speaking to the press than others [...] and you did end up with de facto spokeswomen [...] despite attempting not to.'

Sue Say agreed that there were 'good spokeswomen' when it came to the press who 'often being the straight, Christian, white, and politically capable of speaking, made it easier for the world to hear the cause'. But she added: 'I think they were leaders in their own right, as women, but that didn't mean that we were followers, if that makes sense?'

Perhaps one of the most pleasing twists of fate in the saga of the Greenham women and the media is that Lyn Barlow was actually head-hunted to join their ranks when she left the camp. 'I went to work as a researcher for Duncan Campbell at the *New Statesman*, and that was a result of stuff I'd been doing at Greenham, that I'd passed on to him,' she told us proudly.

7

WEAVE A DOVE INTO THE WIRE

The politics of art

KATE KERROW

Carry Greenham home, yes,
Nearer home and far away,
Carry Greenham home.

Singing voices, rising higher,
Weave a dove into the wire,
In our hearts a blazing fire,
Bring the message home.

From 'Carry Greenham Home', by Peggy Seeger

At almost 100 pages, *The Greenham Songbook* is all at once an odyssey, a covenant and a rebellion, its pages strewn with hand-drawn illustrations of the campaign's iconography, each set of lyrics in a new hand, a new pen. It is a gathering of voices; it is the art of not one individual but a collective. To listen to the few recordings of the songs is to be transported to their camp, to get a taste of the vibrancy of the protest, of the explosion of women's activism bursting from the groundswell of the second wave.

'There were just hundreds of women,' Jill 'Ray' Raymond told us. 'The way that we sang "You Can't Kill the Spirit" – it wasn't a bloody church choir thing, it was actually full of anger and power, and we were voicing our resistance, and it really helped us. Singing helps your breathing because if you're frightened you stop breathing [...] We didn't sing it like a three-part harmony, it was like full of "You're not going to fucking kill my spirit!"'

Remembered as one of the most popular songs at camp, the song evokes the sense of an internal female spirit. Comparisons with the natural world emphasise her eternal power, conviction and wisdom, which is unshaken and steady, an enduring resource. 'You can't kill the spirit,' the lyrics read. 'She is like a mountain, Old and strong, She goes on and on and on.' The connection between the earth and the woman is vivid, echoing the fundamental point of the Greenham campaign – Women for Life on Earth. Equally, it speaks to the women's belief in NVDA; while the women suffer violence from others, they themselves work to survive violence through non-violence, through being in touch with inner resistance and the peaceful yet powerful notion of 'the spirit'.

The women also used the songs to explore women's position in society. In 'Brazen Hussies', they call for the 'fragile image of our sex to die', drawing on the verbal abuse they received for gathering together as women in protest. 'Men call us names to be nasty and rude, like lesbian, man-hater, witch and prostitute,' they proclaim. Then 'What a laugh, 'cause half of it's true!' they sing, exposing the irony of the position of the prostitute; she is a figure supposedly deserving of abuse by the very men who ensure she exists. And in 'Revolution Talk', an Everywoman figure called Jody 'tells her story, she's been raped five times', and Esther, too, 'with her shock treatment, bucking with her mind'; the Greenham women reveal how they 'hold their pain close', acknowledging that 'sometimes it leaves me desperate, sometimes it helps me fight'. The song observes the second wave's success in bringing feminism into academia, but asks that we not hide behind feminist theory and, instead, put it into action:

> You study feminist theory in your university
> Fill your mind with book reviews, and bibliographies
> But when your sister calls you, are you really there
> Or is your sense of sisterhood just rhetoric in the air

The songs also explore how recognition of women's suffering under patriarchy results in harnessing a woman's power to agitate change. 'She changes everything she touches / And everything she touches changes,' one lyric reads, in recognition of the socio-political possibilities that follow self-liberation. Womanhood is perceived as holding ideas about how to do things differently: 'It ain't just the web, it's the way that we spin it,' they sing from their women-only space. The women's 'eyes are bright' when they are at the peace camp, they are 'the dreamers of new visions', they are 'the witches who will never be burned', they are 'the flow and the ebb', 'the weavers and the web'. Under the full moonlight, the imagery is of the women dancing, joining hands and 'joining souls' – championing ideas of sharing and togetherness, reminding us that the earth belongs to both itself and its inhabitants, and not to a selection of political elites. To the latter, they assert: 'This earth is not yours to put boundaries around.' Across many of the lyrics, the women reveal this deep-seated respect for the earth as a shared home and identify with the innocence of childhood – the notion that we arrived undamaged by patriarchal ideals: 'Mother Earth carry me, Child I will always be.' So, too, the strength needed to fight annihilation can be found in both sisterhood and the natural world: 'Sister moon watch over me, Until we are free.'

The songbook also celebrates the concept of change. We see women inhabiting new sexualities and embracing the joy of lesbianism:

> I kissed her and she kissed me,
> And we could see it was meant to be,

Well I used to be a sad woman,
Now I am a blissful dyke.

It encourages us to embrace new approaches to children and child-rearing, recognising the pervasive power of patriarchy to shape young minds. In 'Your Children Are Not Yours', the women advocate the liberation of young minds, asserting that each individual has a right to explore their own ways of being. 'You can give them your love / But not your thoughts,' the lyrics read. 'They have their own thoughts.' This is furthered in 'Yesterday's Children', who are thought to be 'the product of war', and that the children of today are trying to communicate 'that the answer to peace is not a nuclear war'. 'Which Side Are You On?' presents the idea of a dichotomy, asking the listener to make a choice: are you on the side of homocide and genocide, the side of racial strife, the side of the man who beats his wife, the side who 'live the war'? The Greenham women say they seek life, creativity, positivity and peace, and that these values are incompatible with the values of the other side. Against the elitist political drive for complexity, the women's message of simplicity remains powerful.

In the heartfelt lyrics of 'Sarah's Song', we see the determination to fight against external oppression by sustaining internal liberation:

They can forbid nearly everything
But they can't forbid me to think
And they can't forbid my tears to flow
And they can't shut my mouth when I sing.

They can forbid nearly everything
But they can't forbid me to think
And they can't forbid the flowers to grow
And they can't shut my mouth when I sing.

They can forbid nearly everything
But they can't forbid me to think
And they can't forbid the sun to shine
And they can't shut my mouth when I sing.

The women reveal their commitment to the campaign in 'We'll Come Back'; 'They can drive us away / We'll come back, time and time again.' When we consider that not only were the missiles removed from the land, but that the land was returned to the people; that the women suffered relentless violence and imprisonment; that they survived living outside in all seasons; *and* that Greenham was kept alive for almost twenty years, these lyrics didn't boast empty promises.

Folk singer Frankie Armstrong wrote many songs documenting life at Greenham and the campaign's political heart. She remembers, in 1980, being invited to a 'New Moon' party in London in support of Women for Life on Earth. She went along. 'They were feminist and eco-engaged, anti-war. And I thought "that's my repertoire",' she told us. After the party, Frankie was asked to sing and entertain the Women for Life on Earth on the Welsh march in 1981, when they passed through Bristol. She remembers the time as being one aspect of a truly exciting movement: 'I was involved with lots of things in the women's movement in London [...] There were just lots of women around that feminist arts scene [...] We were all kind of networking [...] It was a very exciting time to be part of the women's movement.' Frankie had worked with Peggy Seeger in the Critics Group and she, Peggy and Sandra Kerr had written the first self-consciously women's album in the late sixties and early seventies.

Frankie had already been booked for a feminist workshop on the day of Embrace the Base, and so was unable to attend the protest. Frankie and the workshop organisers, feeling it was unfair to cancel the workshop for all the women who weren't able to attend Embrace the Base, decided to weave the workshop's themes into what was happening in Berkshire that weekend:

We told the people we were going to bear witness to Greenham – write and improvise songs over the course of that weekend, which is what we did. It was a very powerful and moving weekend [...] We sang stroppy songs, we're-with-you-in-spirit songs, you know, songs about our fears – particularly from those who were mothers – fears of the nuclear invasion in this country coming close to home. So we honoured what was going on at Greenham even though we weren't there.

In 1980 Frankie saw a Royal Shakespeare Company production of John Barton's *The Greeks* which she remembered included a wonderful speech to Apollo. 'It was about the dark versus the light and why Apollo was a danger,' she said. After the production, Frankie bought the script, and, as she was losing her sight, asked her friends to read it to her. She remembers the speech advises that Apollo is dangerous, that his light blinds. In her interview, Frankie recited the speech that tells of how Apollo killed the dragon who guarded the ancient oracle for Mother Earth: as soon as Apollo had won the oracle, he began encouraging men to trust only reason and truth. Mother Earth taught instead that truth could come in disguise, and at night sent dreams full of deep reflection. Apollo begged Zeus to take the dreams away in case women became too wise, and so Zeus took away the power of dreams and the nuanced understanding they could bring. Frankie told us:

> I thought it was such a powerful statement – that we only know about Apollo, about the rational. It was a combination of Greenham women and that speech that made me write the song 'Out of the Darkness'. And because I had virtually lost my sight too and I was thinking about all that kind of Christian stuff about the light versus the darkness [...] It really relates to racism too, you know, the dark being equated with the negative evil, the light always with righteousness and the sacred.

Listening to Frankie's performance of the song is to hear the rallying cry of womanhood, the unleashing of a deep, authentic voice which challenges the conventions associated with the woman's voice. In her lyrics, she conveys the power of emotional engagement, the importance of seeking deeper meaning:

> Out of the darkness comes the fear of what's to come
> Out of the darkness comes the dread of what's undone
> Out of the darkness comes the hope that we can run
> And out of the darkness comes the knowledge of the sun.

Out of the darkness comes the fear of the unknown,
Out of the darkness comes the dread of bleaching bone
Out of the darkness comes the hope we're not alone,
And out of the darkness grows the seeds that we have sown.

Out of the darkness comes the fear, revenge and hate
Out of the darkness comes the dread of indifferent fate.
Out of the darkness comes the hope we're not too late
And out of the darkness come the songs that we create.

Darkness is the place of life, darkness is the womb,
Darkness is the place of death, darkness is the tomb.
Death belongs to life, half of day is night,
The end won't come in darkness
But a blinding flash of light.

Bridget Boudewijn documented her time at Greenham through a different art form: photography. She took a great many transporting photographs which reflect the diversity of experiences in the women's testimonies. One photograph shows the lyrics of 'Out of the Darkness' written in a neat, regular hand, across the side of what appears to be an old yellow Fiat. Just as Frankie's performance of the song challenges a more conventional approach to vocals, so the careful hand of the artist, recounting the lyrics in their entirety, challenges the conventional ways in which we see the art of graffiti.

Frankie was at the centre of the surge of creativity in the women's movement in the early 1980s, in which women were championing new forms of creative expression and reinventing the conventional and the traditional. 'There really was this groundswell,' she said. 'I was doing big workshops for women [...] women were all kind of interlinked. So the point at which Greenham appeared, we were ready to join in in whatever way we could. Helping as singers, as lawyers, as women going to Greenham, and those who went to Greenham and wrote poetry and wrote songs, women journalists who went and wrote it up.'

The most famous song to come out of Greenham was Peggy Seeger's 'Carry Greenham Home'. At the heart of her song is perhaps one of the

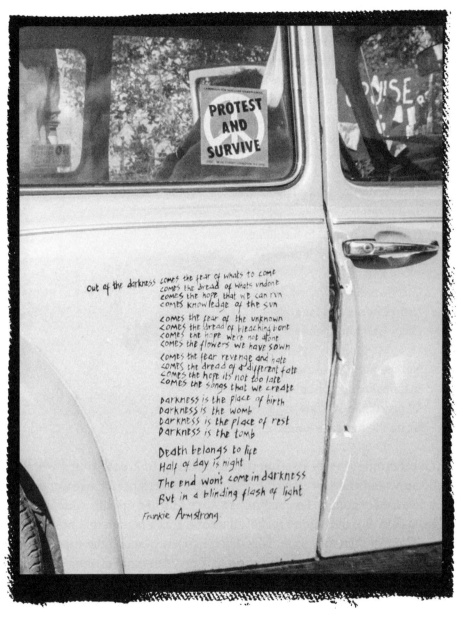

A Greenham woman's car decorated with lyrics from the Frankie
Armstrong song 'Out of the Darkness'. (Bridget Boudewijn)

most important messages of the Greenham campaign: the desire to widen the web, to bring the lessons learned at Greenham into the world outside of the camp. In this way, the women would achieve not just the removal of missiles from the common and the return of the land to the public, but a revolution in social, political and cultural behaviours, bringing mass radical change. This radical change is rooted in peaceful living; in Peggy's words, in the value of the 'loving human dream':

> Singing voices, sing again,
> To the children, to the men,
> From the Channel to the glens,
> Bring the message home.
>
> Carry Greenham home, yes,
> Nearer home and far away,
> Carry Greenham home.
>
> Not the nightmare, not the scream,
> Just the loving human dream
> Of peace, the everflowing stream,
> Bring the message home.

Like Frankie, Peggy used her time at camp to create songs which documented and expressed the power of the experience. 'There weren't a whole load of guitars, I don't think, so when I turned up with a guitar they liked that. But they didn't make a fuss of me as a person that was more well known than they were. That didn't happen.' Among the cups of tea, the sitting around the campfire at night, Peggy remembers moments that might find their way into art occurring all the time. 'So this particular night, there's two or three soldiers with a dog. And Rebecca Johnson is standing – she had flaming red hair – and she was standing holding the fence, and she was singing her nightmare. She was spontaneously singing the nightmare of nuclear war,' Peggy told us, full of awe. 'It was quite extraordinary. I'm a musician, I'm a songwriter. But I don't know that I would have been able to write something like that, much less sing it. And it was musical. And it was poetic. It was immediate.'

In 1983, director Beeban Kidron, then in her early twenties, would take the name of Peggy's song and use it as the title for her first film, a documentary about Greenham. Committed to creating authenticity in the work, Beeban lived at the site with the film's director of photography, Amanda Richardson, for around seven months. Across our interviews, all the women celebrated the documentary as being a deeply authentic portrayal of the world at camp. The film sensitively portrays so many aspects of living at the camp, from meetings about money, to actions, violence, birth and liaison with journalists and photographers. It contains some deeply moving individual interviews with women reflecting upon their intimate thoughts and feelings, as well as their impassioned political beliefs. This interweaving powerfully conveys the conviction that the personal is political.

Beeban's documentation of the actions helps convey the pioneering, creative strategies of the women. Some of the scenes show the women's work with wool, where wool webs would be created as complex obstacles for police to overcome, or used as barriers, or even symbols. Ray reflected on this work: 'If you use nylon wool it's a lot harder to break as well [...] It's very womanly, the knitting and the crocheting and the weaving – we are the weavers, we are the web, we are the flow, we are the ebb. It was an absolutely crucial symbolic thing. The strength of that tiny little thread, you know, it's hard to break.' Ray told us of times when the women were at the magistrates' court: 'We'd go in, try and look respectable [...] then it would start, we'd whip out our balls of wool and we would completely web up the court [...] like throwing these balls of wool across the public gallery [...] it was a really fantastic symbolic thing to do.'

Furthering this return to traditions of creative work with textiles, in 1984 the seventh Boise Quilt was made by the women of Boise, Idaho, and was given to the women's camp. The Greenham Boise Quilt is on display at Lynette Edwell's home in Newbury, and the dedication reads: 'To the women of Greenham Common, weaving and reweaving the web of life.'

'The quilt is both patchwork and quilting with squares,' Lynette said. 'It's made by different women who have used items of personal importance. Items that they would have wanted to place on the Greenham fence for the Embrace the Base action in 1982.' A scroll came with the quilt and stated:

It was made of family clothing: grandma's heirloom lace, dad's fishing trousers, wedding dress, dancing dress, baby clothes. Each family made a square representing things that were precious to them, to emulate the personal precious items which had been hung on the Greenham wire fence by Greenham women and of which they had seen photos and they expressed their solidarity with the Greenham Women's Peace Camp.

As well as its stay at Greenham, the quilt has been displayed in Manchester, on a demonstration outside Manchester cathedral, at an exhibition in Glasgow and is on show on a regular basis at Aldermaston Women's Peace Camp.

'The quilt can be borrowed by any Greenham woman for six months, provided it is always available at short notice for a funeral if required,' Lynette told us. 'One of the most recent funerals where it was displayed was for Toni Brown, at Bristol in 2019. She was a community peace

A textile impression of a moment at the peace camp by artist and Greenham woman Lyn Barlow. (Lyn Barlow)

campaigner, a potter and gardener who helped to establish City Farms in Bristol. A year earlier it was on display for Helen John. I did bring it out for a street party – everyone was going royalist mad and I couldn't join in with their enthusiasm, so declared an anarchist corner!'

Just as textiles were used performatively to great effect – the wool web across the court, the ceremonial bringing out of the quilt at funerals – so *Carry Greenham Home* documents other performative art forms used in protest. One scene shows the women keening en masse – the wailing sound penetrating on a profound level. Many of the women discussed how much keening upset the authorities around them, and how practised the women were at it. The effectiveness of this primal sound of both mourning and pain was a powerful part of many actions, large and small.

Jenny Engledow remembered the women using the old furniture people had dropped off at the camp, and creating a living room with a settee, a lamp and a cardboard box turned into a television. The soldiers didn't quite know what to do with the women as they watched them all sitting around the cardboard box, pretending to watch *Eastenders*, commenting on the storylines. This shows the ways in which the women used their creativity to form bonds, and the championing of creativity for creativity's own sake.

One of Elizabeth Beech's most striking memories from camp is also an example of performative art, and illustrates the power of one individual to make change:

The woman came from Wales, I think – she just sort of arrived one evening. We greeted her, made her a cup of tea and so on. And she had a little tent, and she put up her tent [...] she seemed shy and reticent. We tended not to push women, you know, just let them be. And then at about two o'clock the next afternoon, there was something going on in the base, and she obviously knew that too. And suddenly, just as the gates were opening, she appeared from her tent wearing this most exquisite rainbow chiffon dress. I mean, it really was the most delicate thing – like gossamer. She looked like a fairy [...] She looked absolutely gorgeous, [...] And she just wafted in front of this lorry, and very gracefully sat herself down with her skirts all round her.

She looked exquisite. The whole thing shuddered to a halt. And they were all mesmerised, the police were mesmerised, nobody seemed to know what to do. And then the traffic subsequently backed up to Newbury. And at some point, presumably the police were radio-ing through, they were told to do something. So one of the policemen went up to her and said, 'You need to get up now.' And so she did, she just got up, bowed to the lorry, went back to her tent, took off her dress, came over to the fire and about a half an hour later, she said, 'I'm going now.' And that was that. She'd done what she came to do. And I think it was – that was to me, one of the biggest things, those are the legacies of Greenham, those moments when something like that happened. So magical.

When asked if there was an image that summed up Greenham for her, Elizabeth said it would be the fence during Embrace the Base. 'The fence with all those items on it, the blankets and the baby clothes,' she said. The fence was a work of art in and of itself, containing pictures of children, balloons, letters, signs and banners, teddy bears and children's toys. Some women even tied their wedding dresses to the fence, leaving them there, symbolic of their escape from the trappings of patriarchy. Woollen peace symbols could be seen woven into the wire, and of course, the symbolic web was woven into the fence and woven out of the fence. The use of colour was striking and joyous, juxtaposed against the bleak grey of the base.

In our research, we spent time in the Greenham archive at the Women's Library in the London School of Economics, as well as visiting Lynette Edwell's collection at the Berkshire Record Office. In both fascinating archives, we saw the vast quantity of artwork in the form of banners, badges and zines, as well as paintings and drawings of life at camp. Circles of dancing women hold hands, the sun behind them, the bent and blackened trees curving about them, evoking the wildness of the outdoors. Symbolic images of the web, the dove and the dragon recur, shaping the iconography of the campaign.

Pagan symbolism and images from the natural and spiritual international world were recurring themes in Greenham art, appearing on posters, fliers and the feminist magazines that came out of the camp. (Christine Bradshaw)

Women – reclaim Greenham! pamphlet (Penny Wilson)

One of the most frequently used images was the witch. A symbol that paid tribute to the thousands of women murdered in genocidal witch-hunts across the globe, in the hands of the Greenham women the witch became a symbol of resistance, of reclamation, of women-led revolution. A socially unacceptable figure, the witch resembled all the women who refused to co-operate with systemic oppression in all its forms.

Another repeated image was of two hands with the tips of the thumbs pressed together and the tips of the index fingers together, making a triangular shape. 'It's a cunt,' Sue Say said, when asked about the shape. 'We used to stand doing it, with our hands up towards the gate and the base, and we enthused and centred all our women's energy against patriarchy.'

The image of the spider is widely drawn and woven. Arachne, considered by some Greenham women to be the forgotten thirteenth zodiac sign, was said to symbolise the spiritual and intuitive element of human nature. The connection between Arachne and Frankie Armstrong's source material for 'Out of the Darkness' is meaningful; the dreams of emotional wisdom sent by Mother Earth in the darkness parallel the skill of intuition symbolised by Arachne. In discussing, exploring and using creative protest to expose the atrocity of nuclear war, the Greenham women embrace what Arachne symbolises and Mother Earth promotes in Frankie's source material: emotional engagement. Nuclear weapons are hidden from view, their workings scientifically inaccessible; they are seen as the rational, logical approach to defence. But the Greenham women asked us to find ways to emotionally engage with the horror of nuclear warfare, past and present. Out of the darkness, as Frankie says, comes the realities of our emotional pain – fear and hope, in life and death.

On the badges and banners, these symbols appear alongside eco-feminist witticisms: A Woman's Place is in her Union; I'm one of those common women from Greenham; Protest Resist and Survive; Awake the dragon; Pay women not the military; Cat lovers against the bomb. The zines, coming from a world without perfect computer typefaces, are drawn by hand and act as a reminder of the tenacity of the women – by hand, by telephone tree, by newsletter, by zine, they communicated word of the camp, growing it to that 30,000-strong circle of hands around the base in 1982, and into that almost two-decade-long campaign.

In our conversations, many women reinforced the idea that Greenham was about creativity, and that the women could be free to create without criticism. Everyone was encouraged to have a go at expressing themselves creatively, and find opportunities to be inventive. Elizabeth commented on the investment the women made in their art. She recalls a time when she had been completing a piece of embroidery:

> I remember on one occasion, it was a very lovely embroidery, I'm still not pleased about what happened to this day [...] I used to sit around the fire most afternoons sewing it. And one afternoon, this mod plod [policeman] came at a run, grabbed it out of my hand and ran off with it – it was about three quarters completed. And I was really upset about that [...] I mean, it was quite clever on his part. Because it was really distressing.

The level of emotional investment in the creativity had power: 'I think there was the feeling of doing this action, this sort of ferment, almost volcanic, this energy rising of everybody being there and doing the same thing together – that is a creative feeling,' Mica May said. 'We knew that what we were doing was transitory, that we were making things with leaves and twigs, that they would disappear. And because we were getting more and more aware about the ecological stuff, we were also not wanting to make things that were going to damage the earth [...] we wanted to make things that would be gone easily, you know the quote, "Take only memories, leave only footprints".'

But even under this philosophy, it is possible to leave artistic legacies. Women talked about taking ideas born of Greenham and using them in other campaigns, such as in the anti-apartheid movement, which remained operative in Britain until the early 1990s. Ray commented that she used weaving in a protest which aimed to stop the demolition of a Travellers' site in the mid 1990s, taking the wool to court and creating a web: 'Nobody had ever seen this done. It was a mixed group, and they were younger than me mostly [...] but we did the web weaving there, and it was very novel for them.' Maggie Parks noted that, in 2016, Rape Crisis England and Wales announced a digital project aiming to connect women and girls who had experienced sexual violence through one national resource; they called it 'Weaving the Web'. 'It's interesting how that symbol has carried on after so many years,' Maggie commented.

The outpouring of creativity at Greenham seemed to live on in the hearts and minds of the women; in life after Greenham, the women championed the art of disseminating messages in new ways and embraced creative visions at work and at home. For the women, creativity appeared to align itself with the political; creativity was seen to cure apathy, bring engagement, give birth to original thought that challenged tired and oppressive socio-political systems and, indeed, offered an opposite to nuclear weaponry and its promise of destruction.

8

TAKE THE TOYS FROM THE BOYS

Non-violent direct action

REBECCA MORDAN

Take the toys from the boys
Made a bomb out of cotton
Take their hands off the guns
Made a bomb out of coffee
Take their fingers off the trigger
Made a bomb out of sugar
Take their eyes off the dials
Made a cannon out of water
Get their minds off the money
Take the toys from the boys

From 'Take the Toys from the Boys', by The Poison Girls

With their variety of backgrounds, ages and experiences, the Greenham women disagreed on many things. Much discussion and time was put into establishing what women-only space meant, how different gates would be run and how money, provisions and donations would be distributed and utilised. But one thing unified the camp: the macho arms race that threatened the world must be challenged and it would be done through NVDA.

The principles of NVDA had their roots in international civil and land rights campaigns; many of our interviewees mentioned being inspired by Gandhi and Martin Luther King Jr. Before these movements and closer to home, Anna Parnell and the women of the Irish Ladies' Land League had successfully employed NVDA tactics to start to loosen the English grip on Ireland in the late nineteenth century. The camp was committed to using creativity, non-compliance, passive resistance, collective action, humour and courage to challenge laws they found immoral, and to reject or subvert authority when it acted in bad faith.

The fence was a focus of many of the women's actions, whether they were gathering at it, scaling it, cutting it or rocking it. (Illona Linthwaite)

To do this without behaving like the forces they were opposing allowed the women to lead by example and to discover if it was possible to be the change they wanted to see in the world.

NVDA actions at Greenham took on a wide variety of forms: sometimes they were intimate and secretive with small numbers of women working under cover of night – even one woman talking to a soldier through the fence could be an act of subversion, talking down the walls of perception to find a common humanity. Or actions could involve thousands of women coming from all over the country for a weekend with bands, creches, food and banners – loud, unmissable, unbiddable. The actions could be carefully planned and publicised, or spur of the moment, based on the women's moods or the movements at the base. NVDA was often the basis of actions and a part of larger demonstrations but it was also a camp-wide philosophy that changed how many of the women lived their lives forever.

AROUND AND AROUND ...

'Gandhi said that if you lie down in front of a horse it won't trample you. So we did it, and it worked.'

Janet Smith

Whether at demonstrations, during arrests or on blockades, one of the NVDA tools most regularly employed was non-compliance. As Hazel Pegg explained: 'I mean, you just sit or lie in the road, and refuse to move and they say get up and move, and you just smile. Don't do anything. And then they have to remove you themselves and you don't resist. You just go limp. And they have to take you away.'

Often, when military vehicles were trying to enter or leave the base, any women present would lie down on the road and, ignoring the police's orders for them to move, make themselves as heavy as possible by completely relaxing their bodies as they were dragged out of the way. Sue Bolton, visiting the camp from the Isle of Wight with Ventnor

Peace women, remembered: 'When they were bringing the missiles into Greenham, the actual missiles – a group of us said, "Well, no, this isn't happening." So a whole load of us just laid in the road.' As soon as they were dragged to the side, the women would jump up and rejoin the women on the road, to be removed repeatedly. Annei Soanes, joining actions with her local CND, recalled:

> So we would be like rows of people sitting on the floor, arm in arm [...] we weren't going anywhere. And the police kept trying to move us, and they would peel people away from the edges. And we'd go away, but then we would come back at a different part of it [...] The spirit of NVDA, it's about showing no resistance. It is about being a dead weight, it is about kind of being dragged along the floor, or you know, in other words, not doing anything that represented violent action. It was about the power of non-violence. You know, it was about holding the presence, and saying, 'No'.

Alison Napier, who regularly drove minibus loads of fellow students from Aberdeen to Greenham, told us: 'The main thing I remember about it was just not to resist [...] and then you become a dead weight [...] so the police have to drag you, they've got you underneath your shoulders, your arm pits, and they just have to pull you, and you're incredibly heavy [...] and if they released you a little bit, then you just flopped back down again.'

To maintain this passive resistance and repeatedly place oneself back into hostile hands took courage and fortitude. Alison also recalled that women would be linking arms to support each other and make themselves harder to move. Sue explained:

> We'd learned that when you lay in the road like that, and you were going to be threatened, you have to have an arm around each other, so we're all holding on to each other, so then you don't get scared. Because otherwise if you weren't holding on, and you sat up and looked at what was coming out, you would die. So we're all laying down holding on to each other, and we didn't listen to anything, we just laid there. And they galloped their horses at us. Terrifying. It

was really, really frightening. It was so shocking. And those are the kinds of things they did. So you know, male violence was a very, very big thing. So I was going home and being hit by my husband for protesting. And going up there and having horses galloped over us.

Many women describe the affinity groups that women used to navigate their safety during actions. 'Affinity groups, were kind of action groups,' Janet Smith told us, 'and you'd sort it out at the time, what your role was, and whether you were going to do NVDA or not [...] that was how the actions were organised, people worked in small groups, and those could change [...] I think that was the strength of it – it wasn't reliant on just a few people, or a particular leader, or any of those things.' It was in these groups that women would decide 'who were going to do the actions, and people who were going to observe'. Often the groups would have a legal observer or adviser to witness and note police behaviour and arrest procedure which 'didn't guarantee you wouldn't get arrested, but you're less likely to get arrested, and they would record, the observer would record what was going on, often by taking pictures, but also just by writing things down'. The legal observer would also 'make sure the legal help was sorted out, and a solicitor was contacted, and know the names of everyone'. These measures created a practical solidarity among campaigners and allowed people to take personal responsibility for themselves and others, agreeing with their group to what degree they wanted to get involved with the action being undertaken. A woman might remain in a blockade until arrests were made and then she might stand to the side to take note of the arresting officers' numbers or provide information to friends, family or the press. Alison remembered conversations with her group:

We knew that we weren't going to be violent or fighting back, or resisting arrest, because we knew that we probably would be arrested, and it was made quite clear, or we made it quite clear to each other – this is probably speaking about the Aberdeen contingent again, that arrest was very probable, and if you weren't wanting – nobody wants to be arrested – but if you wanted to avoid being arrested, that was absolutely fine. So it was really important that you take steps to not be in the position where you might be arrested. And there was no hierarchy amongst that, there was no 'Look at us, we're big and brave and tough, and we don't mind being arrested', it was just very clear that everybody was at different points in their lives. I mean if you're a mum you can't be arrested, if you're a single parent you can't be arrested, if you're in particular jobs, you can't be arrested.

Unfortunately, even the best-laid plans did not always prevent arrest or ensure events proceeded without aggression. 'You never knew' whether what you were doing was going to lead to arrest or not, explained Janet Smith, 'because it wasn't really about what you were doing, it was about what the policy was at the time, or how they felt – I guess whether they had a budget!' Having suffered arrest several times herself for different actions as part of the peace movement, Janet told us: 'There were certain police forces who were quite brutal, especially during things like the blockade where we took the fences down. I remember loads of people got our hands sort of battered from them hitting us. They were quite vicious, and they took their numbers off, so you couldn't report them.' However, uniform could occasionally conceal unexpected allies. Janet also told us: 'See the police, I mean some of them I remember on the blockade, I remember a guy showing me a CND badge underneath his lapel, one of police guys.' Sue shared a similar memory: 'We were singing, holding hands on the Embrace the Base thing, and behind us there was this male voice, and I turned around and it was a policeman singing the same songs. And I said, "Oh, it's so lovely to have you here singing with us." And he opened his uniform jacket and he had millions of peace badges underneath.'

Embrace the Base was one of the first and largest actions held at Greenham. 'Embrace the Base – that was really powerful,' Annei Soanes noted, 'because we literally were standing next to each other all the way around the base, and we did embrace it [...] it was surrounded by women [...] And you know, people came from all over the world, it wasn't just this country.' Aside from the women's out-reach, such as the telephone trees, members of CND like Annei and Quakers from all over the UK swelled numbers of attendees:

There was a big Quaker presence there. The Quaker women were absolutely gorgeous. And they were just so peaceful and so gentle, and they were a real big presence there [...] my discovery of the Quakers was at Greenham, was part of the peace movement. Because the thing about Quakers they seem to – they live what they believe. For them, the political is the personal, and they quietly just get on with stuff.

For many women, it was Embrace the Base that brought them to the camp for the first time. Maggie Parks, who would go on to live at Green Gate, recounted vividly how hearing about the mass action and deciding to take part in it unfolded:

People started asking me if I was going to go to Embrace the Base, which was December 1982. And I said, 'Oh, I don't know what it's about'. But [...] I kept hearing Greenham, it was like on the wind and everywhere I went there was Greenham [...] so on the the day before the Embrace, I decided to get in my car and drive there [...] And there were just thousands of women, I couldn't believe it, really. And I was walking down the road. I thought, where am I going to go? How am I going to do this? Where am I going to sleep? And I was walking down the road, and I saw this figure coming towards me, and it was a woman called Carol who lived in my hometown who I didn't know particularly well. But I said, 'What are you doing here?!' And we had literally both arrived independently in our cars. So it was suddenly like I had someone to be with. And if you're going to take part in the action, they wanted you to go and register. So around the base, there were these different tents where you could go and sign up because obviously they wanted to keep track of everybody. And they wanted to completely blockade the base.

So Carol and I headed for the tent [...] There were women with walkie-talkies, there were tables all set up, and the registration forms, and all sorts of things. Carol and I were in a queue to register, and we suddenly heard some women just a little bit ahead of us in the queue talking [...] So we met up with them. And suddenly we just had what at Greenham are called 'affinity groups', because you had to be in a group [...] and there was training, safety warnings, stuff like that. So

For some actions thousands of women arrived at the camp to add their voices to the campaign. (Illona Linthwaite)

immediately, I had this little gang, which was sort of a bit serendipi-
tous, really, and very exciting [...]

And then I remember us actually getting the call that we had actually all joined up. And we were all holding hands [...] And, you know,
I think it was one of the most thrilling things I'd ever encountered [...]
I think I had tried to be my daddy's good girl, even though I was a bit
of a crazy hippie chick but you know, I'd always wanted to please my
dad. And I think I was a little bit in awe of authority and all of that. So
I'm sure it wasn't on that first blockade, but I know on future blockades that I was on – I was on many of them – looking up into the face
of a police officer who was telling you to move and saying, 'No', was
one of the most liberating things I'd ever done, you know, to actually
be confronted by that real authority figure and say, 'No', was quite
incredible. So that was my journey to Greenham.

At these large actions that brought women together from all backgrounds, NVDA was often used creatively to represent the lives,

experiences and concerns of so many different women. Carolyn Francis remembered an action she came down for from Lancaster in 1985: 'There were thousands and thousands and thousands, thousands of women all tying things on this fence. Tying things that meant something to them, about their kids or, or about life generally, and leaving. So the whole place was then, you know, the whole fence was decorated the whole way round.' On another occasion, Sue recalled how even hundreds of thousands of women could work collectively in the moment: 'We rocked the fence down,' she told us, and despite the 'walls and walls of soldiers', she remembered that 'there were people behind us singing [...] and we just rocked it and rocked it and rocked it, and it fell down, loads of it – hundreds of yards of it fell down'. Sue added drily, 'And it was on the telly, because my mother told me she'd seen it and how dreadful it was. I said, "Yes, mum, I was there."'

Illona Linthwaite, an actor and director who was part of several actions at the camp, recalled her favourite one, which called for women to 'Bring mirrors to turn the base inside out, trees to plant, candles for silent vigil, and instruments for songs', as she read to her interviewer from the flyer she had saved. 'This was on Greenham Common, Sunday the eleventh of December 1983,' she told us. 'Well, I didn't bring an instrument because it would have to be a piano and that wasn't practical. But seeds and everything else [...] And the whole fence was surrounded [...] Reflect the Base.' Illona described how 'this particular day was extraordinary' as more and more people arrived and 'all the trees were decorated with stuff [...] kids' clothes, bits of knitting, all woven into the fence'. The women encircled the base with mirrors and candlelit vigils. 'It was a completely wonderful day [...] You know, because it's just that feeling of the power that people have. But I hadn't been on a completely female occasion before, and that was very, very exciting.'

NVDA was used to refute authority without aggression of any kind, and it was the unlikely, inventive irreverence of some of these actions that most confused police and military. 'I think it was the creativity and the ridiculousness of some of the things we did that were actually the most befuddling, particularly to the police,' said Janet Smith. Hazel Pegg agreed, remembering how the soldiers 'didn't know how to deal with grandmothers, didn't know how to deal with mothers with

A young Illona Linthwaite experiences women-only, non-violent direct actions. (Illona Linthwaite)

children [...] I mean, they're in the army, they're trained to fight [...] but they've got bloody grandmothers sitting there with knitting needles and toddlers!' Janet recalled an action where 'we put knitting wool webs across all the gates, got strands of wool kind of going various places, and we were just sort of sitting in amongst them, around the gates, and the police were trying to drag people out, and they were getting tangled up in the wool'. The simplicity of the scheme seemed to further fox the officers: 'I mean, it was only knitting wool, but they just couldn't handle it [...] the police couldn't really work out how to deal with it.'

Capitalising on the confusion that NVDA could create, Gillian Booth took part in an action to mark the anniversary of the atomic bombing of Nagasaki, in which six women stripped off, 'daubed ourselves in tomato ketchup and soot from the fire [...] and then presented at the main gate'. In her account of the action, her friend Hazel told us the police 'didn't know how to deal, they did not know how to deal [...] They couldn't touch naked women!' Gillian added: 'It was brilliant, and in the end they put gloves on!' The six women were arrested and driven through the base where they caused American shoppers to scream when the bus transporting the naked women stopped by the US military's supermarket and the Greenham women detainees of course stood up at their windows. By the time they were delivered to the police station at Newbury, the forewarned officers had 'had to go around various charity shops', said Gillian, and Hazel finished gleefully, 'trying to get clothes for you all!'

Mica May also recalled that 'we had a naked blockade of the base because we thought the police wouldn't want to touch us, which was true'. However, she recounted that 'we kept our boots on in case they dragged us, we wouldn't get our feet grazed, but they would drag you so you banged your knees still, that was annoying'. Also, Mica informed us: 'We had a snogging blockade, because we thought that love would be something nobody could object to – but of course they did.' Yet, undeterred, she told us: 'I was much more likely to be involved in things that had a lightness and a sense of humour about them, and that was the sort of thing I was attracted to, so that was the sort of thing I ended up doing more often.'

Sometimes the peaceful deflection, and assertive rather than aggressive communication techniques at the heart of NVDA, were used to change the course of interactions with the powerful, creating connections, breaking down hostility and sometimes succeeding in changing hearts and minds. Jade Britton gave us two examples of this, showing how emotionally literate, astute, brave and funny the women could be in difficult, or even dangerous, situations:

Jane was there one night, and she was sleeping in the back of the van, and we'd been out somewhere, and when we got back she said, 'Oh god, you know while you were away? Some of the Newbury youth came by' [...] and we said, 'What happened, what happened?' And she said, 'They opened up the van and they saw me there, and of course I woke up when they came. They were just talking to me for a very long time.' She said, 'I was a bit twitchy because I didn't know what they were going to do, but in the end they got back in their car and went off.' She said, 'I just talked to them', and usually you can talk your way out of things – calm it down, and that was true of a lot of things, like the non-violent direct action things.

I remember a woman called Meryl, and the police came along and they were trying to hang on to us, and I think they had Meryl by the wrists or something, and she was going [*singing*] 'Shall we dance?', and she started waltzing this guy around, and he was in hysterics, he just couldn't keep a straight face at all. And so you diffused it – either by treating them as real people, as opposed to something that was being officious and nasty, and generally they responded. You did get a couple of people who were just mean-tempered, or maybe they'd had a bad day, but that's true of anything. But mostly people you know, even on the other side, were perfectly reasonable.

When we asked women to tell us about NVDA, one of the themes that came up was the concept of personal responsibility – of taking ownership for one's actions and how they impact on others. They would often use this self-awareness to try to engage with people who had positioned themselves against them and create connection instead of opposition.

Sue Say told us of her arrival at Greenham as a teenager and an encounter that has never left her:

I was quite determined when I got there that one of the things I wanted to do was walk around the fence [...] And I literally set off from Main Gate – Yellow Gate – heading towards Green. And as you get to the corner, there's a big piece of concrete. And there was a woman sat on this piece of concrete talking to a soldier [...] I just stood there listening to her, and this woman was telling this soldier, 'It's never too late. You have to recognise the abuse that you do. When I abused my children I did this, this, this,' and proceeded to talk about something incredibly personal, incredibly – made her very vulnerable, and she was trying to say to this guy, 'It's not too late, you can change this, I've changed me, you need to change you'.

And I just thought she was so brave, so brave to recognise her own failings, and to use them to try and help someone else to recognise theirs. And I think that that was the single most powerful moment for me when I got to Greenham, was thinking, what is she doing? She's insane. Why would you tell some, some, you know, complete stranger who's not on your side in any way, shape or form – why would you open your emotions like that? Why would you open your vulnerabilities like that? And he massively stood there and abused her. And she sat there so calmly and said, 'That's what I've just been telling you about.' I just thought, yeah, you have – that's a good point. And I think it had so much more of an effect on me than it did him, because it made me see that there was another side to things really, it's always so easy to see when someone's doing something wrong, but to acknowledge yourself and what you are doing wrong, and to try and change it, no matter how bad it is – that this woman was saying, to me, it doesn't matter how bad you've been, you can always change your life, you can always be different. You can always see what you're doing and stop it. And I found that quite powerful.

UNDER, ON AND IN ...

'And you know if you're going to cut the fence, the wires are up here, they're not down here. So you have to stand on the back of another woman. How we did it was a woman would get down like that, and you would climb up on her back. And then you had to snip one, two, three, four wires quickly. And then unravel it. That's how we cut it ...'

Helen MacRae

Of course, not all the women's actions took place *around* the 9-mile perimeter fences of the air base. One of the women's climbs *on to* military property became one of the camp's most iconic actions when it was captured and taken to the press by a photographer.

Since their arrival, the women had watched the bunkers, made of solid concrete and sealed with steel doors, being built in order to house the American nuclear weapons. These silos were much lauded as being the most secure structures on earth, in one of the most secret and well-guarded military bases in Europe. The women decided that early on

New Year's Day, when police and military personnel would be recovering from the night before, would be the perfect time to debunk the myth that the missiles were unassailable, and therefore safe, nestling amongst the local towns and villages in the British countryside. Becky Griffiths described her experience of the famous silo action:

I'd moved down there and very quickly realised there was a sort of plan afoot to go on to the silos at New Year's, the morning of New Year's Day in 1983. And I was desperate to be involved. And there was a big discussion, because we thought they might shoot us – people thought that they might open fire, because we were going right into the heart of the thing, you know, we're going on to the missile silos. So I think nobody knew what to expect. And so there was some discussion about that. And because I was seventeen, there was some discussion about whether I should be allowed. And there was a girl younger than me who was fifteen, so I made the cut and she didn't, unfortunately for her [...] We'd had a whole thing that we're going to put up ladders, throw carpet over the barbed wire, climb up and over. And then just I think run, there was no real plan after that [...] And there was a photo journalist with us who took a picture which had a flash. So we suddenly were possibly spotted. So we all had to sort of go slightly earlier or faster than we'd planned.

I went up the ladder. I remember coming over and hitting the ground, and then just running, and running, and running and not really – I don't think we knew what we were going to do if we got there. We hadn't got a plan. Or I don't remember there being a plan. But we did get there, and we just climbed up on to this thing, and that picture of the women in a circle singing – we hadn't planned, I don't remember us planning that – I just remember it spontaneously happening, because I don't think we thought we'd even get that far. I think we thought we'd get stopped before then [...] they were on us quite quickly, you know, they were already kind of driving towards us as we were running. So we didn't get that long [...] And then we all got arrested and taken to various jails. I got taken to Reading and was stuck in a cell with two women for the weekend. I think they didn't really know what to do with us. And then they charged everybody, and bailed us all. And then yeah, we went to court, three or four weeks later, I think – can't remember – for breach of the peace. And that was the first of all of the actions that I did.

In order for women like Becky to be able to climb the ladders and hold hands to dance on the silos, other women stayed at the bottom to ensure they could get up. Jill 'Ray' Raymond explained: 'I was in a ditch with ladders, there was quite a lot of support – not just the forty on the top.' According to Ray, there were 'early discussions about what non-violence actually meant and the reason [...] we used ladders was because we felt that cutting the fence was violence [...] in those early days we thought, "Oh, we cut the fence, they'll say we're being violent, we're not being non-violent", so that's why we used ladders.' Hazel remembered the same discussions 'about whether or not using bolt-cutters to cut the fence was in fact, an act of violence'. She recalled:

> There were some women who felt that cutting the fence was an act of violence. It wasn't just passive resistance. It was an active act. And there are some women who will still tell you that the reason that women ended up getting rolled in barbed wire by police is because we took the violent step of cutting holes in the fence and then moving through them, and therefore the forces of opposition rose up in barbed wire. It's very complex.

Before very long though, as Ray pointed out, the policy of not cutting the fence obviously 'got reviewed'.

The silo action that shot the women and their policy of NVDA to sudden national fame was one of many actions that started to unravel public faith in the safety and sanctity of the base. 'I mean, we could have been anybody,' said Fenja Hill when talking about actions inside the base. 'We could have been terrorists, anybody could have done it.' Sue agreed: 'What gets to me is that you've got nuclear weapons here, and we – a load of amateur women – are strolling all over your base. We had a woman camping there for about seven days! What the hell? If this was really, you know, if this is the level of security that they have these

Jude Munden, as a teenager at Greenham, employing the controversial bolt-cutters. (Jude Munden)

nuclear weapons under, frankly I don't want them in our country for that, never mind for anything else.'

Sue's experiences at Greenham show the range of ways women interpreted NVDA within the movement:

I think what I realised when I was there was the potential of protest. There are hundreds of different ways of doing it. And I learned very quickly from listening to other women: some women lived at Greenham – that was their protest. They never broke into the base. They never did this, they never did that, because this was their protest. Other women wanted to be more active. Other women wanted to be like camp voice, they were good with the politics, they were good with the news reporters [...] whereas other ones of us just wanted to make a flaming nuisance of ourselves. And that's what I wanted, I wanted to make a nuisance of myself, but I wanted to be creative about it. I didn't want to do the same old thing. I wanted to find something a little bit more annoying, I think.

Acts of creative and disobedient resistance became part of the daily life of Greenham, both the camp and the base, as the women tested their ingenuity to find myriad ways to be both inconvenient and costly to the UK and US governments. Becky Griffiths remembered the variety of ideas: 'From tiny little things where we'd just go and annoy them by cutting holes in the fence, or I think that same year in 1983, we did a teddy bears' picnic on the base, which was on my eighteenth birthday.' She added, laughing: 'I was the back end of a pantomime cow, my friend was the front end, and we just went on into the base dressed up as giant animals, and took a picnic, and had a picnic, and then got arrested. I don't think they charged us, I think they just threw us out.' Janet was also part of picnics in the base – 'we got more adventurous as they got aggressive' – and she agreed that 'they were quite reluctant to arrest people in the base' because 'I don't think they wanted people to know that we could get into the base so easily'. Becky told us:

Sometimes they'd just throw you out because it was too much – too annoying. And also, trespass by itself wasn't really kind of chargeable, I think they could only charge you with something if you'd broken something, or had committed criminal damage getting in. So then they were left with civil charges like breach of the peace, but I think it was just too annoying to have that many breach of the peace cases going through court. So there were lots of little things like that that I think never got charged, or I don't remember getting charged. But yeah, criminal damage – painting things, did a lot of painting of things.

The things that were painted could include runways, air hangars, planes – nothing the women could get near was safe from CND and feminist symbols. While these acts were harmless to personnel, they were costly to the governments who had to fix, repaint and decommission equipment to ensure it was still working properly every single time. 'At one point,' recalled Ray, 'there was a full time team of fence menders for quite a while, because every night there'd be so many holes made in the fence – women were in and out all the time – and also what we did was, we'd make our holes, and then stitch them back together with a bit of wire, and the fence menders would tour the perimeter of the fence, they wouldn't see it, but we knew it was there.' Costs soon mounted for both UK and US governments, and local councils who often disagreed internally about which department or body should foot the bills.

Judith Baron, who had happy memories of living at the small, calm Woad Gate near Blue, told us:

> My favourite action, and it was just a bit daft – I think we went in, it was somewhere near Green Gate. I can't remember exactly. But people, because the Blue Gate was on the road that led to the skip, people used to like often just stop off. And I think sometimes they wanted to give it to us, and sometimes they couldn't be bothered going any further, and they'd give us furniture. So we'd have armchairs and sofas, and someone dropped off the sofa and we already had a sofa and we didn't want it. So we dragged it round – we went in, we had a box, we drew a television. And we took some sweets and stuff, and biscuits, and pretended, and we all sat there pretending we were watching television, and when the MoD came around [...] we said, 'Please don't come into our living room without permission.' And actually they sort of went along with it [...] I can't remember if they processed us or not. But anyway, they kept wanting someone to sign for the sofa, and none of us would sign for it. So they had to keep it!

Christmas seemed to feature as a time of action for the women, partly because of the season's traditional associations with peace, but also because women living at camp over that period felt it was, as Fenja Hill put it, 'always nice to do something morale-boosting, so it didn't have to be political – just had to be fun'. She described Christmas Day in 1984 when 'Rebecca [Johnson] came round in a car [...] and we went round past Red Gate [...] and we got the bolt-cutters and we cut down both sides and let the fence go flat. And then we drove the car in.' They managed to drive all over the base, across a disused runway and through the commissary and housing at the centre, finally making their way out through the main gate:

> They didn't even look at who was in the car because we were going out not in. So they just waved us through. So, as they opened the gate and we drove through, we were like waving and cheering, and they were going ,'Oh my god, what have we done?' And it was just brilliant. It was just really good fun. And we didn't do any harm other than we chopped the gate down, obviously [...] But it was just because it was Christmas and we wanted to do something interesting.

Maria Ragusa shared a festive account about one of the most memorable inhabitants of Violet Gate, in which being in a car also helped to confuse the personnel at the gates:

> The person I remember best [...] was an elderly lady called Elizabeth – who was amazing, and she slept in a bender [...] And she would get up at five o'clock every morning, go and collect firewood and make a fire [...] On Christmas Day [...] she had made – because she didn't live that far away from Greenham Common – she had made an enormous quantity of mince pies. And I said to her, 'My god, who's going to eat all this?' And she said, 'Oh, I'm taking it for the soldiers in the base' [...] We said, 'How are you going to get them into the base?' And she said, 'Oh, I'll just drive in', so she drove in, and because it was Christmas Day, and they had the relatives going in all the time, they thought she was a relative. And apparently, she went into the canteen and started distributing her mince pies to American soldiers going 'peace and love'.
>
> Anyway, they brought her back, and when I got back from my walk they were just bringing her back, and they said, 'We think this is yours' [...] I said, 'You're not arresting her then?' 'Well no, given that it's Christmas Day and she's 104, no.' Anyway, I said to Elizabeth, 'What are you going to do now?' and she said, 'Oh, I'll just go back in', and I said, 'You can't drive in, they've got the number of your, you don't want them to confiscate your car,' and she said, 'Oh no, I'm

not going to drive in,' and I said, 'What are you going to do?' and she reached into the boot of her car and pulled out the most enormous set of bolt-cutters I've ever seen in my life, and she said, 'I'm going to cut my way in!' And she did just that! She was indomitable. Quite batty, but indomitable, bless her.

The women's ability to turn whatever was to hand to their disruptive and often infuriating advantage is clear from Sue's account of one of the times she was actually arrested, having been caught on the base. The police had apprehended her and a friend cutting the fence at Red Gate and 'they put me in the car next to the driver, and then he went to go and get my friend, and I'm looking at this seat and I'm thinking, that seems a bit stupid – you've left that running!' Having manoeuvred herself into the driver's seat, Sue went on to think, 'I wonder if I can learn to drive?' Soon she had 'the policeman running after me down the street, and I'm driving around in a big tight circle, because I don't know what I'm doing!' Finally, the caper came to an end when 'he sort of dived into the car and I just let go of everything, because he's going "Stop!" – so I put my foot on the brake'. Considering that the officer was partly draped on the car at this point, it's easy to understand Sue's rueful recognition that her actions 'went down quite badly'.

Sue also described the spontaneity NVDA actions could have:

I think that's what I learned, was that you could use your imagination and you could use it by sparking off – you'd start talking to women say, 'Oh, it'd be great if we could do this', and then somebody would go, 'Oh, but if we did that, we should do this with it!' And before you knew it, you were off doing it. You didn't have these, these sorts of discussions and let's do that action in four years' time. No, it's like, 'Come on, let's go!'

But the success of these actions often hung on the combination of women involved. Not all went to the Greenham women's plans or advantage! 'There was, there was a certain "character", shall we say, and I absolutely love her to pieces,' Sue told us, laughing:

But she was not the person you took on an action with you [...] She wouldn't really realise what was going on [...] You know, the times that I crawled through the woods, and crawled right round, and sort of heading towards Yellow Gate, literally the woods, so they would not see us approaching the fence. And then she'd go, 'Oooohhhheeruugh', and you'd crawled for hours quietly. And she'd go, 'Where are you women?' and you're like, 'Aaaarrgh! I've just spent two hours crawling through the mud for nothing now!'

Working across gates sometimes separated by miles and without modern technology like mobile phones, the women could suffer from communication failures that hampered their best efforts. 'Someone would come from Yellow and say, "We want to take pictures of something, so you need to cause a diversion over here, Blue Gate",' Penny Gulliver recalled:

So we'd be, 'Oh great', and we'd all rustle out, and you'd all pee – because we'd all have to pee before you went – and then you'd go and you'd break in, and you'd all get arrested, and you'd be sitting somewhere, and you'd go, 'Oh, what's going to happen tonight?' and then you'd find out they'd had a row at Yellow Gate about who was going to take the pictures and then they called it off, but nobody came and told Blue Gate! You know, those kind of things would happen all the time – because it was like four and a half miles to walk around and tell you, because there was no car, so they didn't bother. So we'd all be sitting there going, 'Oh it's going to be hundreds of people here, and this'll be all over the press', and of course nothing happened at all!

Fenja remembered a night when, at about 2 a.m., 'two of us [...] we cut a hole and we went in [...] we went across the runway, and we came to this hangar [...] And this hangar was full of all these military vehicles and things.' Before cutting in, the women had made sure 'we had loads of wool in our pockets, I don't know why we took loads of wool with us, but we obviously thought we were going to do something interesting'. So once inside the hangar 'we webbed this wool – all these different coloured wools across, between all these vehicles in this hangar, and we were wandering backwards and forwards for ages and ages'. However, before long:

> We heard someone coming, and obviously we must have been really tired because our brains didn't function, because we rolled underneath a vehicle, but we took the ends of the wool with us so that obviously then we could just be followed [...] and we could see these feet that these couple of American soldiers like walking around and we could see the ends of their guns hanging down, because they all were armed, and like looking for us [...] and eventually they did find us and hoick us out.

The soldiers told the women off and put them back outside the gates, but even this comically abortive escapade had a serious message. 'What that did show was if we'd been carrying explosives, we could have blown up that whole hangar. It was so easy and we were in there ages before they turned up, and yeah, we didn't, we didn't do anything violent. But what we were doing was showing them just how badly organised and protected these really, really, really dangerous weapons were.'

Gillian told us that at one point the base resorted to a pen of 'guard geese', because 'they were so desperate to stop us getting in'. She described them being 'inside the fence to make noises [...] because you know, for centuries geese were natural security guards, they honk when people come around'. Far from being put off by the presence of the geese, however, the women considered it their duty to liberate them from their unjust captivity, pressed into service as they had been by the military and imprisoned in a cage. 'Basically, several women took it upon themselves to familiarise these geese with themselves, as it were to make friends with them [...] by feeding them, talking to them [...] every morning and every evening they fed them unbeknownst to the authorities and then one morning women [...] took some bolt-cutters and went to the geese.' Becky was one of those women and she described operation 'Free the Geese' to us:

> My mother came to live at Greenham about a year after I had gone there, and she and I, and a group of women, broke into the base one

Women in the foreground gather before an action in front of some of the underground military buildings in the background. (Bridget Boudewijn)

night, because we'd decided we were going to liberate these geese [...] basically, there was this little building site quite near the fence. And it was related in some way to the silos, we didn't really know what – because it wasn't a functioning building when we broke in. But they decided because people kept breaking in near there and painting it, that they were going to put a pen of geese outside as guard, to alarm them. So we broke in, there were three older women, my mum being one of them, and us two [...] who were younger. And so we cut the fence, went in, we'd got these raisins that we'd soaked in alcohol the night before in an attempt to get the geese drunk, so that we'd be able to get them out easily and quietly.

Of course, they didn't eat the raisins. But anyway, we managed to grab these geese. And then at the point that we'd got the geese, and were hiding, the police turned up, and must have seen the tail end of us disappearing, but we were still inside the base. And me and the younger woman got up and walked to the police, and we were like, 'It was us, we just cut a hole in the fence.' And then I think there was sort of muffled goose noises in the background. And we sort of did a whole sort of comedy cough thing. So the geese got out, me and the younger woman who was with me – we were arrested [...] And after that had all died down, the three older women came out the way we'd gone in with the geese, and let them go on the canal in Newbury the next day.

Sometimes a successful NVDA action could be created on the spur of the moment from a mixture of solidarity, gumption and luck. Sue was a part of a large group of women who got caught in the base on the same night that a military convoy happened to have left the base and then later returned to it. When the women were asked how they got in, one of them pretended that they had hitched a ride with the returning convoy on one of the many A-roads surrounding the base, plucking the road number out of the air. 'The story was, well, we were on the A-whatever it was, and we saw this big truck and we put our hands out and, you know, it stopped and we got on it, and we said, "Oh, we're going to Greenham," and he went, "I'm going there – hop in." So we hopped on to this truck, and they brought us into the base.' Usually, the outrageous claim that a member of the military personnel would have stopped and picked up a group of Greenham women hitchhikers and delivered them into the heart of the base would have been dismissed for what it was – 'just a story' – but, as Sue explained, by sheer chance, the woman making up the story picked the exact A-road that the convoy had actually used. Suddenly, the story couldn't be totally disregarded as unlikely, and the women, seeing how they had inadvertently unsettled the questioning officers, played the situation to their advantage.

One of the women was a correspondent for Piccadilly Radio. The woman phoned the radio station up, explaining that she was arrested inside the base the night before. On live radio, the story about how the women got into the base, and the A-road they had used and that the police had been informed, was repeated. This was now something that couldn't be covered up, and had to be acknowledged and investigated by both the British and American authorities. 'Well, that started something else there,' Sue said. 'They had to send someone over from America to investigate it. It cost them [...] because they had to investigate it. They dragged women over the base and said, "No, take it back. Take it back."' But the women, as one, stuck together and stuck to their story:

> I mean, they tried everything to persuade women to make a statement that said, 'We snuck into the base, we cut into the base,' and nobody would. Everybody stuck to the same story – they had to have the Americans come over, because it's American personnel that were involved in the moving of cruise missiles that night, you know, the practice run [...] they had to investigate whether, in fact, their soldiers had stopped and picked up hitchhikers.

Sue finished her story jubilantly:

> That's one of the sort of things that went really well for us because it caused so much chaos. That's what we were there for [...] I learned that the challenge is keeping control. And I think for every time we made the police lose control, we took a little bit more of our own power back. We would always be making a point with it, we would always be pursuing the goal – which was to make as much of a nuisance of ourselves as possible, cost them as much money as possible.

With the women's success at being thorns in the side of the British and American governments, Hazel said: 'We're lucky we didn't get shot.' Talking to us with Gillian, she explained:

> We had to be kept away. We had to be away from where the nuclear missiles were. The minute we breached the outer security perimeter, if we got too close to the inner perimeter, they were actually authorised there. They had a shoot-to-kill policy. They were allowed to do it [...] the violence did occur to them because they were actually under really, really serious orders, as a military, not to let us the reach the second perimeter [...] Well, none of them did. None of us got shot and killed.

190

Gillian agreed, telling us: 'There were men who apparently said they didn't wish to carry out those orders.'

Despite the near-constant actions of the women living outside the base, it is reassuring to know that the personnel of the British armed forces drew the line – even if their own government did not – at firing on annoying but non-violent women who could have been their wives, sisters, daughters or mothers. Perhaps some of the NVDA principles used in discussions through the fence created an understanding which helped de-escalate these risks. Certainly, it must have been hard not to have grudging respect for the tenacity and outright gall of the women. Penny commented:

> When I think about it now, we were running actions from Blue Gate, on at least a weekly basis – sometimes people would be doing things every night of the week until everybody ended up in prison. And I think there was only four of us – in January or something – when you were doing two on, two off – you know, just to stay up overnight because cruise came out of Blue Gate, so it was like, god, shattering. But shattering in a, you know, you're young and you can do that then. You were alive, and it was wonderful.

THE PERSONAL IS POLITICAL

Like its sister phrase 'the private is political', the 'personal is political' became a rallying cry of second-wave feminists from the 1960s onwards. The concept railed against the assumption of the previous generation's belief that keeping women at home sheltered them from the dangers of a public life. Instead, it identified the threats women faced behind closed doors and from being excluded from decision making and creating change. The phrase also drew attention to the fact that women as a disenfranchised group made up over 50 per cent of all human beings. The system that allowed such a large proportion of the planet to be oppressed by the other would need a radical and very public political shake-down to uproot, and women would need to join together across all their personal backgrounds to bring about liberation. By the time Greenham was being set up, women were flocking to the camp bringing these ideas and the practice of NVDA with them from other groups. 'I think [...] the way that women organised in the seventies and eighties was very much like that – it was small groups,' said Janet, 'and small groups where everyone was equal, there weren't leaders [...] this was particularly strong in the women's movement. Also it's just really effective. And it made it much, much harder for the police, because they couldn't arrest one person as the leader.'

Soon women who lived or visited Greenham were taking its principles back into their communities and applying the methods used at camp in other campaigns. Maggie Parks explained: 'There was the idea that we would carry Greenham home, so that it wasn't just what was going on in the base, but what we were doing locally.' After her time at camp, Maggie lived in numerous places, taking her NVDA with her:

> Worcester Women for Peace was still going, but then in Malvern, which was my hometown, we set up what was called a Woman for Life on Earth group [...] and we did quite a lot of actions – there we closed roads [...] We did loads of workshops, we showed lots of films – and then the miners' strike happened, and we had all the miners' wives come, and they were involved. And we were putting on a concert in aid of the miners' wives. So there was this massive sort of political ferment going on, not just at Greenham, but you know, everywhere [...] I remember going to a peace conference in Nottingham. There were women's centres, you know, there was just so much political activity for women [...] So that was a liberation in itself, actually.

Sue Bolton carried Greenham right into Westminster. 'We did this thing in the House of Commons, they were debating cruise missiles. So there must have been about fifty or one hundred of us that met up there [...] from all around the country [...] And we didn't know what we're going to do.' Sue did, however, know that she 'was going to chain myself to something'. Having asked herself, 'How the hell am I going to get in the House of Commons with chains?', she quickly came up with the following solution: 'I put it all in a Tampax box. So they didn't even think of looking in there. I had about twenty-five feet of chain in a Tampax box [...] So I got inside and chained myself to a statue.'

In an action that was quintessentially Greenham, Sally Hay brought camp tactics right into her nice, upper-middle-class neighbourhood:

Up by the station end of Alexandra Palace, there is [...] a bunker. And it is one of those bunkers into which the government was going to put people in the event of a nuclear attack, a nuclear defence bunker. And there was to be an American army manoeuvre that weekend, I don't know how we found out, and it was called Operation Lionheart. Serious operation, and they were going to practise in this bunker. It was to take place in a particular week, so we went up the weekend before – the North London Greenham support group – and macraméd it shut! Then set up camp. And it was great, because we were ever so local – we all lived in Muswell Hill at the time. We had proper tents, we didn't have benders, we had tents because we're very Muswell Hill!

We stayed there all weekend waiting for them to arrive, and when they arrived, it was marvellous because we greeted them, 'Surprise! We've knitted it shut.' And they honestly weren't quite ready for that, and they haven't arrived with a police presence, and of course they can't do anything because they're American soldiers, so they can't actually do anything about British citizens.

Actually, oddly under the US–UK lines agreement act of 1967, which Harold Wilson signed, actually yes, they could, but luckily, they didn't know that – because they aren't lawyers. They're American grunts, basically. So they asked us [*adopting American accent*], 'Ma'am, go away, and take the knitting, and the fretwork and all' – and we said, 'No, no, we're fine. Thank you. We'll stay.' Anyway, eventually, it was worked out, and they got some equipment and they removed the knitting. And they went in, whereupon we knitted it shut again. I mean, obviously they can get out, because it is, after all, only yarn. But it was very jolly, and it made the local press, and it rather made the point that there is a nuclear bunker under Ally Pally.

Janet remembered going and sitting outside a recruitment office and handing out leaflets about how dangerous it would be to start a war in the Falkland Islands. This peaceful and simple action ended in an arrest that gave her 'bruises everywhere' and landed her and her six friends in 'the prison cells for several hours'; it just happened to be the same day that the British Royal Navy's nuclear-powered submarine sank the Argentine ship *Belgrano*, killing 368 people.[17]

The authorities soon found they could take the women out of the camp but they couldn't take the Greenham out of the women. Sue told us about a group of about twenty-five Yellow-Gaters being taken to Newbury racecourse after an eviction 'because there were too many of us to be held at the police station'. Finding that the room they were in had a bar, the women were soon annoying the police by hopping behind it and serving water to each other (in the absence of any alcohol). A further investigation of the room soon revealed windows that swung out

Yarn and wool were regularly used by the Greenham women to create webbed actions and to confuse the assembled authorities. (LSE Women's Library)

and, as the room became stuffy, these were opened. Within about fifteen minutes, several of the women had escaped on to the racecourse:

> We were running around, the police following and chasing us round – we're going up and down the humps, round past the rails where they do the racing, we were running up and down. We had these police absolutely going mental [...] I couldn't run for laughing [...] because they were getting so uptight and so cross [...] This one particular policewoman was chasing me for quite a while [...] And so I would run, and she would chase me and then she would slow down. So I would stop, and I'd let her catch up a bit, and then I would run off again, and that really annoyed her [...] In the end, I ran back and climbed back through the window [...] we were messing about, no one was making a real escape [...] They could have just stood there and said, 'Look, stop it women,' and probably we would have stopped, but because they chased us in the way that they chased us – because one or two of them were furious [...] Well, furious policemen is just lovely for a Greenham woman, isn't it?

The women proved that their support of each other allowed for spontaneity, to feel fear and take action nonetheless. Sue Bolton never forgot the importance of overcoming fear:

> There was a lot of fear about [...] this overwhelming fear that just eats you up. It's there all the time. I can feel it now. And the minute, the very second, you take a step to change things, the fear goes – the split second you say, 'I'm not having this.' And even if I just stand on that corner out there and say something, my fear will be gone [...] So when we got together and started to do things, it was so empowering. It was just, the fear was gone. It was amazing.

One of Sue's memories perfectly encapsulated her point:

> We had a really amazing children's party [...] It was on May the first [...] So we had the cake and we had maypoles and we told all the kids to bring scooters and bicycles, and we cut the fence, and we went on

the runway and ran up and down with balloons [...] having a blast and singing songs and holding hands. And then suddenly a huge coach turns up, so we all get frog-marched into the coach [...] with our kids [...] And then they drove to a gate and they wanted to chuck us all out of the bus. There were lots of women around the fence by the gate, and there were a lot of police there. And the police got us out of the bus and put our arms up behind our backs and started hitting us [...] And all the women were along the fence, they started to sing, 'We can see you, we're watching you, and we know what you're doing.' And they stopped and they let us go.

Sue explained why she felt the policemen stopped: 'It's that witnessing thing, which is what the whole thing was about, witnessing the crime that was going on worldwide. These women at the gate witnessed that they were hitting us and trying to break our arms.'

Albert Einstein's assertion that 'violence sometimes may have cleared away obstructions quickly, but it never has proved itself creative'[18] is much championed, but rarely are constructive options for this creativity offered. The women offered a solution in their use of NVDA; it could be swift, responsive, careful, compassionate, considered, uplifting, meaningful, impactive, frightening, funny – and it was very, very creative. 'I very much identified with much of what was being said by radical feminism,' Annei Soanes told us:

It made perfect sense to me. Actually, we do live in a patriarchy, there is lots that we're unconscious of. It's not until we start looking at what systems are in place, what we believe about ourselves, what we believe about men, that we can start to address that. And Greenham was a place where feminist politics was discussed, and I can remember being judged harshly by people who were not involved. They would see it as odd. It would almost be dirty.

You know, it was almost like I was doing something to hurt the rest of society. When actually, what I was doing was doing something about equality, about justice, about non-violence, because the conclusion I reached was that feminism for me [...] feminism goes hand in hand with non-violence. And I know that there are feminists who would not agree with me on that level. But for me, that's what it means. It means how I hold myself in the world, how I interact with other people, how I leave my footprint, really. And without my experience of Greenham, and talking about feminist politics in that context, without the women-only space, I don't think I would have had the freedom to talk about it, to thrash out ideas.

9

WE'RE A CIVILISED NATION

Acts of violence

KATE KERROW

Women locked in prison cells.
Nothing to do but cut themselves.

We don't torture, we don't torture
We don't torture, we're a civilised nation
We're avoiding any confrontation
We don't torture, we don't torture

From 'We Don't Torture', *The Greenham Songbook*

'You can't use violence to get rid of violence (...) All it does is create continuing spirals of violence (...) It's about power, it's about patriarchy, it's the nature of capitalism.'

Josetta Malcolm

To memorialise one Nagasaki Day in the early 1980s, a group of women travelled to a clearing full of pebbles, rocks and rubble. For weeks, they worked together to collect and hand-count 100,000 stones to memorialise those lost in the nuclear attacks on Japan. They filled the camp car with buckets of stones until its body creaked and strained under the weight. Then, dressed in black, the women went to Newbury and walked around the war memorial in silence, the police watching them. Soon after their arrival, vigilantes began shouting abuse at them, and then launched a physical attack on the women, who, aligning themselves with the principles of NVDA, remained peaceful. Despite this, the women were arrested for breach of the peace; even more unjustly, while the vigilantes were free to go, some of the women received prison sentences.

Despite many women talking to us of positive police and military relations, this story of the police enacting punishment on the women for *enduring* violence stands alongside a wide variety of accounts which refer to police and military harassment and abuse. The accounts are further supported by Beeban Kidron's *Carry Greenham Home*, which reveals concerning footage of the relations between the police and the women at various actions. Watching the film again, Jill 'Ray' Raymond was reminded of the women's commonplace experience of violence. 'I was really shocked myself at how brutal it was,' she said, adding that the police and the bailiffs treated the women in such ways 'for ten years or more'.

Tamsin Clayton described police behaviour to the women at night as deeply problematic. 'We'd all be sitting around the fire playing, you know, singing or whatever,' she said. 'And I remember one particular time, there was a couple of kids asleep around the fire and they [the police] came and they just threw dirt on the fire, and all the sparks went all over the children who were lying in nylon sleeping bags, you know, and they could have been burned. It was like a really violent thing to do to us.' She added, sadly, 'But I think it was probably a damn sight safer than anywhere else I've lived.'

However, the women were rarely able to prove incidents. Lynette Edwell expressed how much easier she felt it would have been if the women had had mobile phones and were able to record what was

At larger demonstrations the local police force and the MoD were supplemented by other branches of the constabulary. Behaviour from the different police varied greatly, according to the women. (Jenny Engledow)

happening to them. 'I have never witnessed behaviour like the police at Greenham,' she said, explaining:

I had such a bad kicking in the back of my neck, I have a dislocation between my head and my spine, and he didn't have an ID number [...] It put me in a collar for two weeks [...] They really took it out on the Buddhists, because I think they thought they were skinheads. Even the older women were thrown about [...] I think women felt that they didn't count, that they weren't entitled to police protection.

The stories of violence kept coming. Sue Say told us that 'Some of them would sort of pick you up when you were in your Gore-Tex sleeping bags and throw you, kick you, punch you. You know, there was a lot of quite nasty stuff that went on,' while Penny Gulliver remembers the army riling the dogs up so that they were really frightening: 'People got hurt, they got bitten.' Sarah Green stated: 'I was manhandled by the police very often. I think I just became normalised to it.' Mica May remembered her knees being scraped against the ground as police dragged her from various actions.

It seemed, Alison Napier noted, that from early on the local police were out of their depth. So 'they brought in the Met', she said, telling us:

They came in on horses when we were all sitting down doing non-violent direct action. We were just sitting in the road, and they galloped their absolutely massive, massive horses towards us, and then they would scream to a halt very close to you. Very, very frightening [...] They were violent, and they could be violent because we had no means of identifying them [...] I would be very surprised if any police officers were ever reprimanded for excessive aggression and violence. They were very rough, and they pulled women very roughly. They pulled women by their earrings, which gave me a real shudder. I don't wear earrings, but the horror of that – that was awful to see.

Some women also recounted tales of abuse during arrests. Penny described witnessing disturbing interview processes where women were shouted at, had things thrown at them, were dragged about, or one woman would be separated from the group and taken away. 'The first time I was arrested, there were lots of us arrested and they put us all in four or five cells, and they put one woman in a cell by herself [...] they did those kinds of things [...] they would say horrible things through the door [...] If you said anything, they felt very happy to embellish the story with everything and anything they wanted.'

The first of Josetta's numerous arrests came when they were 18. 'I was arrested within a couple of days of ever going there,' they said. 'And for sure, as one of the very few people of colour, I was the first person to be arrested in a whole group of people doing the exact same thing.' Josetta was put in a prison van for hours. The vans were filled with tiny cubicles and several women reported troubling feelings of claustrophobia. 'I had air, but no windows – it was like being in a box [...] I didn't know how long I would be in there, what was going to happen to me.' But Josetta remembers the sense of camaraderie when other women joined them in the van: 'As soon as other women came in, we could talk and we could sing, and that was always the thing that we would sing – we'd learn songs and we'd sing.' On this occasion, Josetta was left in the van for so many hours that the judge didn't sentence them.

Lyn Barlow described being physically manhandled on one arrest, and despite remaining peaceful, she was charged with assault on a PC. 'It just did not happen,' she said. 'I was incredibly upset about it.' Speaking with some members of the MoD police, she said they expressed sympathy and shock, and a constable and a sergeant later contacted her to say they would come to her defence in court. 'They were willing to say that from all their interactions with me, they had never experienced violence. They showed up for me at the court case in uniform.' The case got thrown out.

Lyn recalls Christmas cards and connections with the MoD police, from individuals and their families, explaining that some of them were like colleagues, people of a shared world. In her experience, the Americans were much more aggressive:

It was much harder not to react to that aggression because it was extreme. The British soldiers might not have been sympathetic but they had been told how they should behave. And most times, they followed that. There were incidents though, with British squaddies [...] But I remember two women from Yellow Gate set up a temporary camp between Yellow and Green Gate beside the fence. And they were there alone one night, and the lights along the fence went out, and they were attacked by men in balaclavas with clubs, and they were badly beaten – they both got taken to hospital. And it was a British squaddie who witnessed part of it – he actually called the ambulance and police [...] Until this day, we think they were American soldiers.

Lyn felt the Americans were even more affronted by women challenging the patriarchy than British squaddies. 'I don't know, maybe that's an assumption on my part. But it was the gung-ho attitude, the "We're helping Britain out and look how they're repaying us", you know?'
Remembering one particular night, she said:

We got found by an American soldier outside the control bunker. And we were sat in the front of a vehicle, and they were very protective of their vehicles, you know, toys for the boys. He went crazy. He dragged me out really roughly. And I really kicked off when I was arrested, I wanted to know his name, his number – I wanted to push for a complaint against him. You couldn't, you couldn't touch those American soldiers [...] When Heseltine visited Greenham, there were fences around the silos, three lots of fences. And American soldiers were in the inner sanctum, and women were told if they ever got through that inner sanctum, if pushed, they could actually shoot. It never happened. But if you did get close to silos on an action, you'd see Americans pointing their guns at you.

Tamsin recalled her experience of guns at Greenham:

I did have a gun held to my head once, which was pretty terrifying [...] I later learned that evidently there was a prize for the first person to shoot a Greenham woman amongst the American Air Force [...] We'd gone into the base one night, because we used to do it just to show how easy it was to do it. And we'd done it a few times and not been caught, but this time we were caught. And we were like, running through the base and suddenly we saw all the lights and we knew they were coming, and we were like, 'Oh my god, there's nowhere to run', because we were in the middle of nowhere. And they pulled up and jumped out of their cars and had their guns over the car doors. And they were like, 'Stop, or we'll shoot.'

Now, your natural reaction is to run. The last thing you want to do is to stop, and obviously it's the most terrifying thing that you can ever imagine. And I couldn't stop. But, I just walked slowly, because everything in me told me that I had to put some distance between them and me [...] They ran up and they went *wham* and kicked my legs out from under me, and I went *smash* on to the floor. And then they took us to right around the other side, to Yellow Gate, and kept us there and interrogated us [...] I gave a false name and they weren't that interested in who we really were. They knew that that wasn't my name, and they just kept us there, and then they let us out, and then we had like, miles to walk round back to Red Gate [...] Having a gun held at you is not fun, and you've got no idea how you're going to react until it actually happens. But believe me when they say, 'Stop or I'll shoot', and I see it on telly, I think ummmmm, yes, I understand when people don't stop.

Sue also reported an incident with a gun:

I had one particularly nasty experience with an American military man who handcuffed my wrists the wrong way round, who was trying to drag me all over the place and he pointed a gun to the back of my head when I was on the ground, and said, 'I'm going to shoot you'. And this was just after we'd been told we'd be shot and I thought, well, if I'm the first, I'm the first. But as it happened, we ended up with British Ministry of Defence police coming over and saying, 'You know, that's one of my citizens – unhand her.' Which was brilliant.

Feeling that there was a potential drug problem in the base, Josetta told us:

I remember coming across a squaddie with very bloodshot eyes and a gun, on Salisbury Plain in the middle of the night. They would exercise vehicles and do manoeuvres in the night, so we would do actions at night [...] And that's why part of our actions were always about singing, because women singing makes it obvious we were women, and that we were the Greenham women, which they were used to. We'd been doing it since '81.

Despite many of the soldiers being used to the women, Fenja Hill learned about some of the soldiers' fears about the women themselves. 'They were told such crap about us,' she said, explaining:

How we all wore razor blades inside the collars of our clothes, so that if they grabbed us, they'd rip their hands to pieces [...] That we were evil witches who would cast spells on them [...] If they saw us as human beings that would be a problem, so some women made huge amounts of effort to chat to them at the fence [...] I recognised how hard it was for the women who did [...] We used to say things to them like, 'If the nuclear button gets pressed, there's nowhere safe for you to go. You might have been told that you're going down into a bunker together, but that isn't going to happen.' If they were going to believe us, that was going to tear at the roots of everything about their lives. So it was quite hard, I think, for them to believe us.

The relationship between the police and the women took an even darker turn in August 1989 when 22-year-old activist Helen Thomas was killed by a vehicle towing a police horsebox outside the base. She had been crossing the road to post a letter. While courts ruled it an accident, Helen's family, friends and many Greenham women have argued against the verdict, stating that police procedures weren't properly followed.[19]

The relationships between the women and the authorities didn't end at arrest. Of the women that we spoke to, a huge number spent time in custody, and in prisons around the country. The initial moments of being in prison nearly always included strip-searches, which Sue described as horrifying and humiliating: 'Putting your arms up, being stripped off with people sitting typing in an office next to you, and all you've got is one little curtain that they pull across, and they made you do star jumps and all sorts of things, and then they make you bend over and look up your bum. It was the most horrendous thing I'd ever been through. I just didn't realise that's what they did.' She laughed and added: 'And as for what they made you wear, that was just criminal – these nighties with little, tiny flowers on them and pink knickers, oh please, it was awful!'

Sue told us she was part of a prosecution team created to take action against the MoD; she says the group put forward a case that unlawful strip-searching had taken place on a regular basis. She remembered:

> They were prosecuted, they were found guilty of it, and forced to pay compensation [...] They were strip-searching us to humiliate us [...] We took a case against them, which we won and a precedent was set. And now strip-searching is not allowed to be done in the way it was [...] They were trying to say a personal search wasn't a strip-search [...] That was, I think, one of the biggest things that came out after Greenham.

Women recounted being terrified in one particular prison, not just by the strip-searches but, as a small number of women explained, by the threat of internal examination. This was said to be happening around the early 1980s, and was conducted by a male doctor in a cellar underneath the main prison building. But the Greenham women had researched their rights; they warned their women about the examination and that they could refuse it. Refusal had to be accepted by the doctor. The supposed aim of the examination was to assess if the women had sexual diseases and, if they did, they could be treated before going into the prison. Nevertheless, the experience was reported as violating and hard to refuse; watching non-Greenham women who entered the prison system not knowing they could refuse and ending up enduring the experience was reportedly heartbreaking.

Women also discussed being put at risk from other prisoners who were mentally unstable, sometimes being shut up in cells with women who were a real threat, engaging in screaming, banging and fits which could be set off by any number of noises from a baby crying in the Baby

Wing or an argument outside in the corridors. Several women reported being shut in cells with women who had serious mental health problems, and some even had confessions from prison guards that they had been put with unstable women deliberately. Perhaps this was seen as a suitable punishment for the Greenham women's disregard for authority; perhaps it was used as a deterrent – a technique to arouse fear and submission in the women for the duration of their stay.

In our conversations with the women, the evictions were repeatedly connected to violence and abuse; while the women reported the day-to-day normality of them, many also reported the high levels of aggression.

'When someone says "Greenham" to me, the thing that flashes into my head is the bailiffs,' said Ray. She remembered the evictions being one of the key reasons for Night Watch. Night Watch functioned as a group of external supporters who would come and guard the resident women while they slept at night. The Night Watchers were able to raise the alarm should the bailiffs come at night, spreading word through the camp by sending a woman from one gate to another, passing the message in the way a relay team passes a baton, creating an alarm system which alerted the women to pack up their belongings prior to the bailiffs' arrival. 'They had a full-time team of bailiffs [...] they were vicious,' Ray told us. 'Dark glasses. One of the first shootings of schoolkids was in Hungerford, and turned out that the guy who went on to do that was one of our bailiffs – that's the kind of level we were dealing with in the bailiffs.' While the information isn't confirmed, Ray wasn't the only woman to believe that Michael Robert Ryan, the perpetrator of the Hungerford Massacre on 19 August 1987, had been a former bailiff at Greenham. Ryan shot sixteen people dead, including his own mother, at a series of locations before turning the gun on himself.[20] Lynette commented: 'The Hungerford killer was widely thought to have been one of the bailiffs.'

Lyn had moved to Greenham full-time by the time of the mass eviction in 1984. She remembers not only how much the bailiffs must have cost, but also how abusive they were to the women. 'They took pleasure in it. They were awful [...] You couldn't form any dialogue with

Rather than letting the police tear down her bender at Yellow Gate, Becky Griffiths set it on fire. She recalls that it felt like an act of empowerment. The lines of police can be seen in the background. After that, the women had more temporary structures. (Paula Allen)

the bailiffs because their sole intent was to disrupt and demoralise.' Lyn recalls one incident with Rebecca Johnson, a long-term resident of Yellow Gate, who was holding on to a piece of her property that the bailiffs wanted to put into the muncher. 'She wouldn't let go of it. And a bailiff had hold of the other end. And they went to put it in the muncher and Rebecca, you know, steadfast, was, "I'm not letting go of it." And they turned it on and it caught the top of her hand.' There was a substantial injury. 'Rebecca fought tooth and nail to get them held accountable for that. She took civil action against them.' Lynette emphasised the damage to Rebecca's hand: 'I believe she has a disability with the hand to this day.'

By 1984, Lynette said the women were experiencing five evictions a day. 'By that time, the evictions were really heavy [...] They took everything and damaged everything [...] Local police would come and watch the evictions. They never did anything for the women.' Tamsin Clayton recalled the repeated phrase she heard many of them use: 'We're not political, we're just doing our job.' But 'they pulled the tents down and poked the benders apart', Alison Napier said, telling us:

> They were trying to clear the site. I mean that was their job, they were doing their job [...] But I think my abiding memory of it was just the viciousness of it, and the petty cruelty of it. They had a fire extinguisher and they would put the fire out. And I think fires are such symbolic things, aren't they? [...] And there were stones around the fire, and they would kick the stones, and I thought, 'You really hate us. Why do you really hate us?' They just left a scene of devastation and off they rumbled to the next gate.

The evictions weren't the only reason for assembling Night Watch. The women, sleeping in the dark, unforgiving terrain of the base, were at risk from violence from varied sources. Reports of night-time violence enacted upon the women by passers-by, vigilantes and authorities appeared across the women's testimonies. Lynette said she wasn't able to talk with us about the individual incidents of sexual assault she knew of that occurred on camp, but she asserted that sexual assault was common: 'There were always cases of women having their breasts fondled and sweaters deliberately pulled up.' Fenja said it was common for youths to come at night and slash tyres, but that there was also a man who tried to sexually assault her. 'Men like that thought that because there were only women there, we were desperate for a man.'

'Women never felt safe at night, which is why we said men are welcome to visit during the day, but not at night,' Lynette told us, explaining:

> There were really two groups of vigilantes in the town. One came from taxi drivers, they used to meet and plan [...] They would defecate in women's tents [...] appear in black, very frightening, throw stones, use air guns [...] And then we had the others which were far more threatening [...] Rebecca Johnson had blood and maggots thrown at her tent [...] We had that fear [...] and the darkness. And the fact that police aren't going to protect you, the military aren't going to protect you [...] There was a phase of women being beaten up [...] six

months to a year. Two very young girls sleeping at Green Gate had the tent come in on them and they were kicked and kicked [...] Two other women were attacked. They had to go to hospital. They were very badly frightened.

Lynette remembered that one of the women was partially blind and, though it was dark, the woman's blindness enabled her to know who her attacker was. She knew he had come around the fire and sat with the women before. Lynette took it up with police complaints and pursued it over time: 'One of the things I regret is that I never got a prosecution.'

'In the diaries, there are endless reports of vigilantes,' Ray said, commenting:

It would say *'viggies' came by in the night and they set fire to the sofa,* or *'viggies' came by in the night and all the tents and vehicles are covered in eggs* [...] The fire service would come and they would absolutely soak our fire pits, so there was no dry wood. People would take our kitchen pots [...] The hot food runs would come and they would bring in the backs of the cars and the vans in straw boxes, pots of stew and stuff to feed us, because we couldn't cook. So that was a really important part of the support, a lot of CND groups did that – Oxford and Southampton [...] There would be perverts hanging around the shit-pit so we had to go in twos [...] cars would drive by and chuck stuff out [...] Because we had the publicity, men knew where we were [...] Some of them might have got reported, but the police weren't on our side [...] But I think we have to remember it's actually not unusual for women to be coping with male violence – for a lot of women, it wasn't anything new [...] we just developed tactics of self-defence.

Night Watch really helped the women to feel safe and to monitor activity inside the base, but it also served as a consciousness-raising activity; in recognition of the need to stay safe, women began discussing their experiences with violence and sexual violence. Among stories the women shared, Ray remembered some talking of becoming pregnant by their fathers, meaning their mothers had to pretend the baby was theirs; generally, when the women communicated their stories and realised they weren't the only women to experience what they'd experienced, they developed a deeper awareness of the scale of the abuse that women were suffering.

Elizabeth Beech told us that, given the relationship between the women and local residents was so fraught, there were worries about going into the town for fear of antagonism. She recalled an incident which many believed was attributable to a local resident. 'We had people throwing lighted torches into the tent area. You know, really dangerous stuff going on. We had a very big fire on one occasion, it was very scary [...] We weren't sure if there had been anyone in the tent that had been burned to the ground.' Tamsin also spoke of fearing going into the town. 'I mean, obviously women had to go to the shops,' she said. 'That in itself could be quite traumatic, because people were very, very horrible. I can remember once being in the laundrette, washing and drying our clothes, and you know, this guy threatening to smash our faces in, and calling us filthy, and spitting on us. So going into town was quite traumatic.'

In December 1984, 29-year-old Deirdre Sainsbury, known to her fellow Greenham women as 'Dee', was supposedly hitchhiking on the South Circular Road in Roehampton. Police found her mutilated body near Denham Golf Club in Buckinghamshire. Colin Campbell was sentenced to life for murder, but his conviction was reduced to manslaughter after he claimed that epilepsy had caused him to attack Dee.[21] Sarah Green told us how deeply the camp had been affected by Dee's death:

It was a terrible time. I'd actually seen her that morning. She wasn't hitchhiking. That was the thing. She was at Victoria coach station, she was getting the bus back, because I just arrived off a bus. And then she was found dead because they said she was hitchhiking. Well, she wasn't hitchhiking as far as I knew. And nothing about that ever made sense. [...] That could have been any of us. It deeply affected us all. She stayed most of the time at Blue Gate. People were absolutely devastated. I remember a lot of screaming. And a lot of celebrating her life as well.

As well as photographs and other objects of affection many Greenham women and visitors to the camp left messages and questions on the fence. (Bridget Boudewijn)

Between 1986 and 1987, a larger number of women became concerned about the possibility of 'zapping' at the camp. The idea of the American and Russian military using microwaves as weapons was topical news. A 1980 US Army report discussed a new experimental practice which would involve exposing people they needed to control to low-level microwaves which could immobilise, harass or tranquillise as desired. Zapping could also take a more direct form in zap guns being developed, which used radio frequency signals and microwaves to destroy, burn, zap aircraft or missiles or varied enemy military targets.[22]

The women we interviewed were strongly divided on whether or not zapping occurred at the camp. Some felt it wasn't occurring at all; others thought it possible that, given that there were many electronic systems at the base which transmitted radio frequencies, the zapping was inadvertent. A large number of women felt they were being experimented on so that the military could work out whether controlling large groups of people was possible through zapping. Considerable numbers of women began complaining of headaches, irregular periods and various illnesses which caused aches, dizziness and overwhelming lethargy. Lynette felt the Green Gate women were most affected by the zapping. 'They decided to evacuate, just leave it totally,' she said.

Elizabeth was sceptical:

It was claimed that this was a deliberate attempt on the part of the military [...] Some women were in wheelchairs and really ill and going public on it [...] Some women from Green Gate came up to Yellow, and explained their distress about it. More and more women said they were being zapped. It did actually have a very negative effect on the camp. Lots of women left.

It was at a time when the camp was in difficulty anyway because we'd already had the incursion by the King's Cross women at that point [see p. 63]. In about '88, I was living in a squat in Hackney and I had a call from Channel 4, about a programme called *After Dark*. The researcher said to me, 'I understand you don't believe in zapping?' and I said, 'No, I don't believe in zapping.' They asked me to take part in a programme with a woman who said she was affected by zapping, and someone from the MoD who would claim it was a psychological experiment on the part of the MoD [...] I said, 'Yes, of course, I'd be really interested.' And it was due to take place in a fortnight's time. Then, programme pulled, never heard of again. Nancy Banks-Smith, very famous television critic, wrote a huge article saying, 'This is one of the best programmes on television. Why is it being pulled?' And nobody's ever, from that day to this, explained anything about it. And I've never had an opportunity to say anything about it. But I thought it was really, really interesting.

Alison, who sadly died shortly after our interview with her, discussed her brain cancer with us. 'I was diagnosed with cancer three years ago, then it went away, and now it's come back. And you find yourself thinking of all the different things that might have contributed to that over the years. I would never stand up in a court of law and say, "I was zapped in 1983 by the US Airforce and therefore, you know, I'm not very well." But it was a very shocking, covert aggression towards what was a peaceful protest.' Whether or not the claims of zapping were founded, they certainly reflect the sense of aggression and intent to harm that the women experienced at times from the authorities.

The women's stories of violence and abuse were shocking in content and number, especially given that violence was so often the chosen response to the women's non-violence. The Greenham women voiced their concern that the earth, belonging to each and every person, was under threat of obliteration by the few; they voiced their anger that they were expected to care for and protect their children from danger while simultaneously calmly allowing them to live in the shadows of annihilation; they asked that the money society put into violence be put into international aid which could improve the lives of so many living in poverty; they asked not to be murdered; they asked not to be poisoned; they asked for us to learn from Hiroshima and Nagasaki. In return, the women endured cycles of violence and abuse in various forms across their entire campaign.

10

WE DON'T LIKE YOUR CAUSE

Law and disorder

KATE KERROW

We don't want your laws
We don't like your cause
We won't fight your wars

From 'Chant Down Greenham', *The Greenham Songbook*

That the women ended up in the court system and spent time in prison wasn't just an unfortunate consequence of the campaign, but a direct part of their strategy. Women spoke of plans to fill up the prisons and to challenge patriarchal behaviours in the judicial system. They aimed to expose the ways in which the system blocked the path to peace and nuclear disarmament, and to reveal its misogynistic treatment of women.

One of the key reasons that the prisons became full was because when it was possible for them to do so, many of the women refused to pay fines for their release, instead choosing to serve their sentences. Alison Napier discussed the empowering nature of refusing a fine and standing up to the system:

> You just stand up for what you know is right [...] to what is effectively the state, and in this country that's all the state will do to you – they will try to take your money, and you say, 'No', so then they'll take your liberty, and you say, 'Well, okay,' and then who's won there? It's an incredibly empowering thing [...] You can just not be cowed by what the state is telling you to do [...] To realise that you can break a bad law, and retain your power, and say, 'Well okay [...] you put me in a box for five days, and then I'll come out of the box, and I'll do it all again.' It's like nothing the state can do can ever actually frighten you again.

Following one of her arrests, Alison and her cohort were sentenced to seven days for trespassing and then non-payment of fines. But Holloway Prison was full of Greenham women. 'They had to hold us in the cells underneath Newbury police station,' she told us. 'It was actually illegal, it's not meant to be used for detention.' She recalls that the press mostly weren't interested despite the alleged illegality, but the *Morning Star* apparently publicised that the women were being held illegally. She remembered a small cell with nothing in it other than a tiny glass strip of window and a narrow bed. Alison said they spent twenty-three and a half hours a day in the cell, and then for half an hour each day, they were allowed outside to walk around a yard. 'I knew I was going to prison, I had no intention of paying the fine [...] I'd taken Doris Lessing's *The Golden Notebook* with me to read, which was really big and thick.'

The Greenham women used their campaigns, court cases and even the fence around the base to draw attention to injustices and discrepancies in the law between rich and poor, weak and powerful. (Bridget Boudewijn)

Of course, Greenham women came in solidarity to support their imprisoned sisters and stood outside their cell; as the cell was at basement level, the window strip allowed the inmates to look out on to the pavement. 'The women would stand outside singing songs, going around and around Newbury police station. It was just fab. It was just astonishing.' She laughed, remembering that they all got out after five days for good behaviour: 'There wasn't a lot we could do to be bad!'

Most of the women we spoke to had visited Holloway Prison several times across the Greenham campaign. Almost all of them spoke of the fear of the first time, the sense of isolation, the terror of the realisation they were under the control of other people. Janet Smith described her memories of feeling isolated: 'I remember thinking about how far away you are – you looked out of the window and saw a bit of wall, then barbed wire, then another wall, then another wall. It's a long way. You're very far away.'

Inside, women learned tricks of survival like splitting one rationed match into four with smuggled-in pins for cutting, and how to cope with the intense heat. Several women reported the heating being turned up very high in prison, believing it was done deliberately to keep the women quiet and sleepy. There were plenty of little cruelties living on the inside – reading a book only to find the last few pages had been ripped out, or, when on hunger strike, being taken to the shop to watch as the other inmates spent their tiny allowances on treats. Despite this, women reported that the inmates offered increasing support to the Greenham women, recognising the importance of the cause.

While the women comforted one another in this way, it was distressing to see how much mental ill health there was on the inside. From the so-called 'Muppet Wing', where the women with mental health issues were kept, there was regular noise of women screaming, making clear their anger and distress at the physical restraints being placed on them. Lynette Edwell had direct experience of the 'Muppet Wing' after being held there, as, again, the prison was full at the time she was due to serve her sentence. Of the wing, she said: 'It was awful because the women were banging and shouting all through the night. In my opinion, the women were sedated [...] we were offered non-prescription drugs to get us to sleep [...] Our beds had faeces on them.' In a later BBC interview, Lynette discussed how badly the women were treated.

Fenja Hill was told that she could avoid prison if she left Greenham forever. She boldly refused the offer and entered Holloway. In her testimony, she spoke of her strong impression of the poor mental health of the women inside. She remembered the prison was laid out very like a hospital, and she was aware that her cellmate was mentally unstable: 'I just really wasn't prepared for that kind of environment.'

'I've never not eaten in my life,' Penny Gulliver said, explaining:

But I didn't eat for the first four days in prison. They put me in a cell with the only woman I met in prison who should have been there because she was up for four or five counts of GBH – really quite nasty stuff. She was really someone with very poor mental health, and she immediately said, 'Don't speak or I'll kill you'. So I didn't speak in the cell for the fifteen days I was in [...] But almost everyone I spoke to when I was there, shouldn't have been there. They were in for petty theft – food, nappies, that sort of stuff. So many women with poor mental health, so many women who were there because they wanted to get away from violent relationships on the outside. Really the only woman I felt like probably needed to be in a cell on some level was the woman in our cell! But it wasn't the place for her either [...] It was all nonsense. The psychiatric wing was above us and people just cried and wailed and it was awful – all night and stuff.

Penny remembered getting out very little; the lack of oxygen in the rooms caused by the windows being only 2 inches wide meant she spent quite a bit of time with her lips pressed up against the window, desperate for fresh air. 'There were days and days and days when you didn't get out at all and you just had your food put through the door.'

Lyn Barlow spent her childhood in foster homes, suffering from bullying. 'The first time I went to prison, I was absolutely terrified,' she said, telling us:

I think because I had all those stereotypes in my head about what the other women were going to be like, what the officers were going to be like, was I going to be bullied like I'd been bullied by girls when I was in care? And as soon as I got to prison, all that was just obliterated – all those stereotypes.

Yeah, there were aggressive women. But there was no stereotype of what a woman prisoner was like. And I found I could relate to these women, because they'd had similar backgrounds to me [...] a lot had gone through extreme poverty, or domestic violence, or abuse as children. They'd been forced into committing offences because of the conditions that they were living in.

And not only that, women in prison, women who went before the courts were punished on two levels – they were punished for the offence that they'd committed, but they was also punished because they were seen by the male patriarchal system as having betrayed their sex, as having betrayed femininity. So you'd find that women got sent to prison

for offences, quite minor offences, that men wouldn't receive a custo-
dial sentence for – like shoplifting, prostitution, non-payment of fines.
But when I first went to prison, I had all those stereotypes in my head.

Lyn observed a 'stark contrast' between the women in prison and the
Greenham women prisoners, and began to feel a sense of disillusionment. 'I felt – not all Greenham women by any means – but a lot of
Greenham women who went to prison saw themselves as political
prisoners, and didn't acknowledge that the vast majority of women in
prison were political prisoners. And there was a demarcation between
Greenham women, and the other women prisoners. A lot of that was
broken down the more often women went to prison. But it was still there.'

On her last sentence, Lyn found herself moved out to a semi-open
prison. She remembered a time when she was scrubbing floors beside
a Black woman prisoner whom she'd known from her time in a care
centre in Sheffield. 'You know, I'd met her in a Remand Assessment
Centre when I was twelve years old. And here I was in prison alongside
her [...] I formed bonds with other women at that prison, who made me
question specifically, class, I suppose, in a lot of ways [...] the amount of
kids who'd been through the care system, like me, who ended up either
in prison, or in the military, you know, in institutions.'

The recognition that 'as women we learned so much from other
women', and the strong bonds she made with women in prison, drew
Lyn to focus on penal reform and campaigning against women's imprisonment. Working as a journalist, she began to smuggle out women's
stories and raise awareness of what was happening to women on the
inside, and how what happened to them on the outside contributed
to them ending up on the inside. The movement for women's prison
reform would begin to gain traction in the 1980s partially as a result of
Greenham women coming out of prison and telling the stories of the
inside. But like many of the women who endured time in prison, Lyn
felt she couldn't do it again:

You look at the rise of nationalism, popularism. You look at the way
that people like refugees and asylum seekers are demonised, this
culture of hatred. And I think, 'Is it about time that we once more

became activists?' I couldn't take part in NVDA anymore, I couldn't put myself in a position where I would get sent to prison. I could no longer do that. But I think the time is coming when we've got to re-group as women, young women, older women, mixed groups, everything. It's coming to the point where we've got to listen to our conscience and try and do something to effect change.

Penny described a key learning from her Greenham days as a recognition that 'there's a whole load of women in prison because they're poor women – that's why they're there'. The powerlessness of being in prison was striking to her, reinforced by having to call the prison officers 'Miss':

It was like none of the women should be here, and isn't that enough – that you lock them up? But once they're there, it's a bit like you're absolutely being ground down into the dirt, to make you as submissive and as powerless as they possibly can [...] and everybody was on drugs – everybody had stuff given out at night, and it was a bit like on so many levels this is so wrong, and it was awful. Awful to see [...] And anybody who was pregnant – none of them seemed to hang on to their pregnancies when they were in there. Yeah, awful.

Janet Smith reflected that it was one thing to know how people in prison were disadvantaged, but another to see it. She remembered how living in prison, in lockdown, suppressed the emotional distress of the inmates, which frequently led to dangerous or violent outbursts and mini-riots. 'I remember one breakfast that I was at where someone upturned the table and people started getting up and waving their arms at each other, and officers just rushed in shut everything down, and kicked everybody out, and sent everybody back. So those kind of things were just kind of normal.'

Although Sue Say remembered doing eight or nine stints in prison, her belief that 'jail was for real criminals' was broken down on her very first visit:

When I first got there, I went into a dorm. The night before a pair of scissors had gone missing. And there was this woman in the cell with

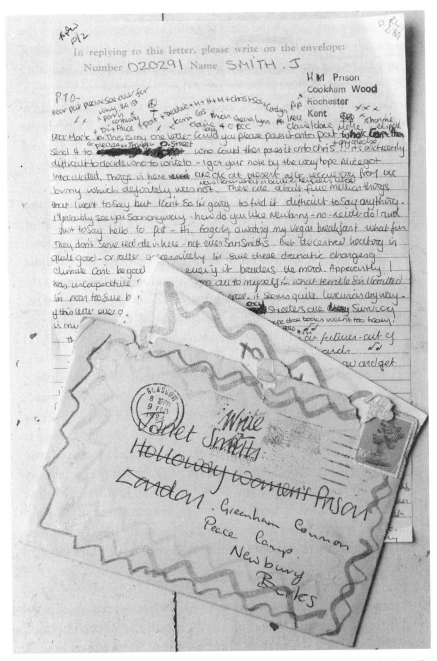

The Greenham camp was so recognised that Janet Smith was able to write letters back there from her cell in Holloway Women's Prison. (Janet Smith)

really long arms, and all the other Greenham women shot over to the other side of the cell, because she was saying, 'Oh, I hate Scousers, – you know me boyfriend was a Scouser, so I stabbed him to death.' So Lesley, who is pure Scouser, went over to one side of the room. Stella went over to the other side of the room, and Muggins gets the bed underneath hers. And I spent all night with my back against the wall, watching, forcing my eyes to stay open, watching for this crazed lunatic woman whose arm was going to come round and slice me with this pair of scissors. Right?

In the morning I was like, 'Oh, I'm hungry' and she was like, 'Here, have my breakfast!'. As it happened, she was having a laugh at our expense. Actually, what she'd done is she'd walked down the street, seen one of those rails of leather jackets and thought, 'Oh, it's not pegged down to the ground,' and wheeled it around the corner, and there was a policeman there and she got caught. So no, she hadn't murdered her Scouse boyfriend at all. But it woke me up.

The other woman in the cell had stolen a pint of flaming milk off somebody's doorstep. She was hungry. She had nothing and she nicked a pint of milk. She'd been there eight months on remand [...] And it was just like, what in the hell? I expected these to be crazed, lunatic women. And I'd gone in with that in mind and realised they were women just like me, they were women just like the women at Greenham. They were just women. And they had had a lot of unfortunate things happen around them. And one of them was in because the police were using her to try and get her boyfriend to admit to a crime that he'd committed. It didn't take me very long to realise that I'd had this illusion that crazed women who killed people would be the ones in jail. I think there was only one person I met in jail who I thought belonged there, maybe two.

Sue grew to realise that women were in jail because of abusive relationships, poverty and addiction. Rather than the women being the 'bad folks', Sue felt it was mostly the wardens. She watched how they treated the women, the way they would put newcomers on wards with women with mental health problems to frighten them. 'They put me on a deportation wing once,' she told us. 'I woke up with a whole load of women around my bed shaking it. Greenham women weren't doing what the authorities were telling us to do, so they were putting us in dangerous situations – they were prepared to do that.'

In fact, as Sue noted, this backfired, because the Greenham women got to learn about what really happened inside, and began taking it on as a political issue. While there, Sue was not only part of the important legislation which challenged strip-searching, but also part of organising hunger strikes, a singing protest and a rooftop protest. 'It was a bit of a shocker, I think,' Sue reflected. 'Having to manage women who didn't care about their authority [...] We were awkward. We were difficult. We made it hard for them. But that in turn made it easier for the other prisoners, because they were focusing on us instead of them and I think we did quite a bit of good in there sometimes with that.'

After her first time, Sue wasn't frightened of prison any longer. She grew more concerned about the way people were being treated in prison than about being there herself. She remembers the women in prison had a working network to check on each other's safety; people would pass messages round to find out where people were. 'We used their network to make sure that women were okay. Particularly if somebody had been hurt when we'd been arrested and nobody'd seen them. Then we'd ask around and people would pass messages and we'd find who was okay.'

On one of her prison visits, Sue remembers an ongoing conflict with a prison officer which began when she refused to sign over her property on entry because they had unfairly taken a photograph from her. She and her friend were thrown straight into a cell. The officer then refused to let them go to the toilet all night. In the morning, she brought breakfast for the two women. 'I drank the tea and as I got to the end, I felt something strange against my lip. She'd put all her nail clippings in it.' Sue didn't go near the breakfast she had left for them, but her friend ate it all on purpose. 'It had been left out that long it was congealed to the plate [...] You could pick up the paper plate and turn it over and nothing moved.' When the officer came back in, her friend had eaten it all and commented on how delicious it had been. The officer 'actually screamed [...] that for me was the moment [...] driving her to that point of actually screaming [...] she was trying her hardest to get us'.

While the stories of poor treatment in prison were pervasive among the women we interviewed, Fran De'Ath's experience reflected how the women sometimes did manage to break through the authoritarian relationship and develop a point of positive emotional connection. The police came to arrest Fran on one occasion. 'They all knew me,' she said, recalling one specific memory:

They'd all been for tea in my teepee [...] It was very beautiful, my teepee. And there is nothing like an open fire, you know [...] I've got a lovely big brass tray with my teapot and my cups and saucers, and it's all full of beautiful rugs. It was lovely [...] So they used to love coming. And then they say, 'Oh come on Fran, we're going to have to arrest you.' And I say, 'Yeah, I know.' And they say, 'Stand up, Fran and walk into the van.' And I say, 'No, sorry lad, I can't.' So they very gently had to carry me off and put me very gently into the police van, and off we go down to the police station.

Fran De'Ath and the police at a Greenham blockade. (Fran De'Ath)

So we get there, and everybody says, 'Oh, hello Fran!' And after a little while a policewoman comes and says, 'I'm very sorry Fran, but I will have to do a search now.' And I say [...] 'All I've got on me is my tobacco' [...] and I pulled my tobacco out of my pocket and she said, 'Oh that's all right, search is done then.'

Down in the cell, the pleasantries continued:

Next to it there's a door open and it's a bathroom. I said, 'Oh, maybe I'll just nip in and use the loo' [...] So I go to the loo, turn on the taps, wash my hands. I said, 'Ooh, hot water out the tap, it's so nice, isn't it?' and she laughed and said, 'Well, would you like a bath?' I said, 'Ooh, yes, I'd love a bath.' She looked at the bath and said, 'Oh, it's a bit grubby, isn't it?' So me and her scrub the bath together.

So I'm in the huge, deep bath [...] then there was a male cough. Then, 'I thought you might like this, Fran.' Under the curtain, tucked under lovely soap and shampoo [...] Clearly nipped out to the shops. 'Oh, thank you very much,' I said. So of course I'm in there, I'm loving it [...] And the woman, she says to me, 'Fran, I'm awfully busy. Do you mind if I just go and leave you and when you're finished, will you just pop yourself into your cell?' I laughed. I said, 'Yes. I'll pop myself into my cell.' [...]

Later the chap comes along and says [...] 'Would you like some lunch?' [...] So after a little while, a slot opens in the door. And it was on a tin plate with melamine cutlery. But it was a lamb steak, with red wine sauce, with the most delicious vegetables [...] When they came back for the plate, I said, 'Well, that was very nice – not at all what I was expecting.' And they said, 'Well, we've had your hospitality. We didn't think you would like the police canteen food. We popped up to the local hotel and got it for you.'

Just as the women deliberately undermined the authorities in the prison system, they refused to be obedient to hypocrisy and injustice in the courts. From doing their own cross-examinations and self-defence, to bringing cakes into court if a birthday arose on the day of trial, the women used a variety of non-violent, creative methods of protest.

Elizabeth Beech was once arrested for taking a 12ft crucifix into the base. 'The court case was more amusing than the actual event as they claimed not to know what I was carrying – on Good Friday.' Outraged by the fact that the authorities had placed an illuminated 'Peace on Earth' sign above the silos, Elizabeth borrowed the crucifix from Catholic Peace Action, decided to carry it into the base and read right through *The Passion*. She ended up at Newbury police station, and then was later dropped back off at Blue Gate, despite the policeman knowing she was from Yellow Gate. As such, she faced a 5-mile walk around the common back to her home. This was a frequent tactic of the police when taking the women back to camp after arrest. Elizabeth then waited some three months for her court case.

In court, Elizabeth cross-examined a young squaddie, asking him to describe the object that she had brought in. 'He had huge difficulty with that. He said, "It was very big, was very tall." So I said, "Well, did it resemble anything to you?" So he looks at me as if I were talking Chinese. I said, "I mean, did it look like anything you'd ever seen before?" He said "No!".' Elizabeth was given a conditional discharge: 'The magistrate said it was on the grounds [...] that this soldier seemed incapable of recognising a very commonly understood object, which made him nervous for the security of the nation!'

Mica May was part of campaigning with the Women in Prison group, with which Greenham women became connected when they began seeking prison reform. On one occasion, they had set up a small protest camp outside Holloway Prison. 'This one policeman was being really petty about us being there,' she explained. 'We'd moved stuff so that people could walk by, but he was doing us for obstruction.' One of the woman called him 'a wanker', and he managed to get her taken to court for it. 'In court,' Mica said:

This woman said to the judge – I think it was a judge, not even a magistrate – she said, 'Your Honour, I did call him a wanker.' The policeman had said she'd shouted it. She said, 'I used the same tone of voice that I'm using to you. I do have a voice that carries, but I don't ever have to raise it [...] And to call somebody a "wanker" is merely saying that they masturbate. Who among us had not masturbated?' And the judge went *Bong!* and the case was dismissed!

On one charge for obstruction, Alison Napier decided to appeal using legal aid, and felt she ended up radicalising the local solicitor who represented her. 'My case was that it wasn't me causing the obstruction. I felt nuclear weapons were causing the obstruction, and if that wasn't going to fly, then the police themselves were causing far more of an obstruction than we were. All I had done was sit down in the road while they drove nuclear weapons through the gates.' With this argument, Alison managed to win her appeal.

On New Year's Eve 1982, in response to the Secretary of State for the Environment Michael Heseltine's reported assertion that RAF Greenham Common was the most secure base in Europe, a large group of Greenham women climbed to the top of the missile silos, held hands and danced. Photographs and video footage of the women in their circle of sisterhood, silhouetted against the cold, winter sky and the barbed-wire fences, were highly impactive at the time, engaging the humanity of the public. Barrister Elizabeth Woodcraft remembers watching the women dancing on the silos that New Year's Eve when it was broadcast on the television. The footage moved her. But at the time, she had no idea how deeply involved she would become in the campaign.

In 1983, Elizabeth, who had come to the Bar specifically to work for women, was instructed to represent the women at their hearings in Newbury. She went to several meetings to talk with the women, to give advice and to work through some of their issues. The hearing on this occasion was to decide whether or not the women had caused a breach of the peace. Elizabeth knew they would more than likely be found guilty of breaching the peace and, as such, were then going to be ordered, or bound over, to keep the peace. Then the women would refuse it, and would therefore be sent to prison.

'But the women wanted to use the hearings as another part of their campaign,' Elizabeth said. 'We were merely lawyers – we would tell them what was possible, what wasn't possible, and if they did such and such what the outcomes would be.' But a lot of the time, the women didn't tell Elizabeth and the team what they were going to do. 'They all came into court and began singing every response they made to the magistrate in the style of a Gilbert and Sullivan opera. These were lay magistrates,' Elizabeth laughed. 'Just the good and gentle folk of Newbury, and they didn't know what to do.' The magistrate would ask their names, and the women would sing them back, and they'd get sent down to the cells. Every now and then, the magistrates 'would advise to check if the women were ready to come back upstairs, and they would check, and the doors down to the cells would open and we'd hear them singing again, and then the doors would close'.

Elizabeth also remembers the other ways in which the women flouted authority in court: she recalled one saying in deliberate irony that she did agree to be bound over to keep the peace because that's all she was trying to do in the first place. Additionally, the women gave themselves different names ('one woman called herself "Isaac Hunt" [...] say that very quickly!'); one woman came wearing a red-dyed tampon dangling from the centre of her beret; on one occasion, when they called the Commander of RAF Greenham Common to give evidence, the women all jumped up and performed a citizen's arrest on him for his conspiracy to commit genocide.

Working with a team, Elizabeth tried to develop a defence for the women. Eventually, they decided to pursue the line of self-defence. 'They were acting in [...] a way to try and defend themselves, their families, their children and the rest of the world from this dreadful risk of cruise missiles and nuclear bombs. We all knew what happened at the end of the Second World War with Hiroshima and Nagasaki. And so that's what they wanted to prevent because they knew what the effects of a nuclear bomb could be.' The additional element of the defence was that the Americans had used A-bombs in the Second World War, and nuclear weaponry had advanced since then with the second generation H-bomb, capable of far greater destruction. They also looked into the implications of the Genocide Act, using key components to build the women's defence.

Due to the nature of the defence, the women almost had carte blanche on which witnesses to call. Elizabeth recalls witnesses giving evidence on the making of bombs, including a South African barrister who gave evidence about conditions in the mines in his country, where they were mining the uranium required to make bombs. The defence explored

Young barrister Elizabeth Woodcraft, sitting on the far right, with colleague Isabella Forshall in dialogue with the Greenham women with whom they were building a defence. (Sarah Booker)

human rights abuses across the whole process of creating the weapons. 'It was an extraordinary thing,' Elizabeth said of the whole experience. She believed it was the first time a defence of that kind had been used in such a way in the British courts.

In a later case where some women had been arrested for demonstrating on top of Holloway Prison, the women on trial used the court hearings as an opportunity to expose conditions in prison. 'It wasn't just about nuclear bombs, it was also about women's position [...] just talking about women's lives, what's important in women's lives, how women are treated [...] It was wonderful.' Of the women, Elizabeth said: 'They were incredible. And so brave, I mean, so brave, because they knew they'd be going to prison. They knew that would be the result, and you know some women went to prison time and time again. That must have taken a tremendous toll.' As time went on, the women's press coverage increased. 'It was at a time when there was a lot going on [...] the Thatcher years [...] we were building up to the miners' strike, the anti-apartheid movement around Nelson Mandela. It was close enough for a lot of people to remember Hiroshima and Nagasaki.'

Other legal successes included the challenges of how women could remain living on the site. The idea for a bender came not just from the need for speed under the duress of evictions, but because there were legal challenges to the women living in caravans or tents. One court case appealed for a person to be able to vote with the bender listed as their address. Eventually, the courts decided people could vote from a bender; Elizabeth said she believes that law still stands.

The women even took their brave, tenacious approach to the law overseas. In 1984, thirteen Greenham women and their children brought forward a lawsuit against Ronald Reagan, the then President of the United States, which charged that the deployment of nuclear missiles to Western Europe from the USA violated both international law and the US Constitution. The courts dismissed the case on the grounds that the nature of executive decisions on foreign policy were political, not judicial.[23] While ultimately unsuccessful, again the women had demonstrated their use of strategic and inventive ways of raising awareness, and many argue the continued pressure of the campaign was a contributing factor towards Reagan and Gorbachev signing the Intermediate-Range Nuclear Forces Treaty in 1987, which ultimately led to the removal of the missiles from the common.

After the missiles left, a small group of women stayed on. They had already begun investigating the ownership of Greenham Common, and found legal irregularities which they would take all the way to the House of Lords, asserting that it was still common land. 'They started a chain of action,' said Lynette Edwell. 'And they got the common back.' In 2000, West Berkshire Council took ownership of the land, and it became a wildlife and conservation area. While this time it was not the Greenham women but the council who took the bolt-cutters to the fence to free the land, it was the women who wrote Greenham Common into history, radicalising an entire generation, and restoring rightful ownership and natural habitat where once there was only the promise of nuclear destruction.

11

TOMORROW

Greenham's legacies

REBECCA MORDAN

I'm not here to waste my time,
I'm not here to beg or borrow.
I'm here to claim what's mine –
I'm here to claim tomorrow.

From 'Tomorrow', by Peggy Seegar

'Could never be bothered with all that King and Queen shit, you know, I want to know what people did. And protest history is important and women's history within that is important because that is people's history.'

Becky Griffiths

When we focus on Greenham Common Women's Peace Camp, the view is a seething mass of hopes, fears, struggles and dreams. But if we pull back far enough then three broad, overarching common aims become visible: to see the back of the nuclear missiles housed at the Greenham base; to see the parts of Greenham Common illegally held by the military returned to the people of the UK; and to end patriarchy. The fact that, bloodlessly, the women saw two of their main aims fulfilled marks their campaign out as a protest success story. The knowledge that this success is possible fuels others to continue the struggle against a sexist, oppressive world to create a kinder, fairer, more interesting one. The personal journeys the women took after Greenham – into work, relationships, their communities – represent the legacy of the camp and show how the women determinedly took the political, social and cultural discoveries made at Greenham into the wider world.

Karen Fisher, who went from living at Main/Yellow Gate to co-forming Rebel Dykes and playing a formative role in London's queer cabaret scene as it developed in the early 2000s, reflected on her time in camp:

We always must stand on the shoulders of giants, and so you need to know who your giants were [...] Yeah, I mean, it saved my life. And it changed my life. And I think it did that for all of us, actually. I don't think there was a single person that lived there that wasn't very fundamentally touched by the experience. And there's never been anything like it since [...] I think that's what's so beautiful about it, really, about preserving it [...] It's better to do it now, while we've all still got our marbles!

JOBS FOR THE GIRLS

Sue Say observed:

> I think Greenham gave me the confidence to be a woman – to be who
> I was, and recognise that that's not always going to be the same as
> someone else. And actually, I might have to slow it on down and have
> a look at the women around me, and try and support them in who
> they are. And I think that it taught me some really good fundamental
> skills that I then went and applied in other areas of my life.

For most of the women who spent time there, Greenham was a formative experience born out of concern over the state of the world. It is
therefore surely not a coincidence that many of the careers they created
for themselves after their time at camp had significant social impact.
Sue went on to become a social worker and run a self-insemination
group to help same-sex couples and those who could not afford private
programmes to conceive.

Social work was a popular career choice among the women we interviewed. Sue Lent went into this field, later specialising in working with
disabled children. In 1989 she was also elected as a local councillor, a
role she still holds in Cardiff at the time of writing. When asked by her
interviewer if she thought her experiences at Greenham had impacted
on these career paths, she stated unequivocally, 'Yes, I would say definitely.' Alison Napier first became a social worker, and then later a
lecturer training others. Alison was convinced that she was set on this
course by the relationships she had at Greenham:

> When I was at Greenham, I met an awful lot of very incredible
> women, and one of the incredible women I met was called Naomi
> Griffiths [...] And she also went to Nicaragua and worked as a health
> educator there, and I went out with her on a couple of occasions. And
> so that all came from Greenham [...] Yes, Greenham, the people I met,
> the values I encountered and absorbed. I hope I had a lot of those
> values already, but I think they got crystallised. I've always been proud

that when I apply for a job as a social worker, and I have to write down if I've got any criminal convictions, I, of course, say, 'Yes I have!'

She laughed and added: 'I was at a lovely job interview, and my criminal convictions were on a piece of paper, and I had it with me, and the person interviewing me asked to see it, and I handed it over. And she said, "Ah, yes, me too!" And the whole job interview spun away, and we were just speaking about Greenham.'

Just as Alison was changed by the journeys of others, through her the legacy of Greenham travelled on and extended out. 'My mum was amazing,' she said:

She was a primary school teacher, a very conventional, respectable looking person – tweed skirt, and flat shoes, and a nice handbag, and a sheepskin jacket, and she always incredibly supportive [...] She had a CND badge that she wore on her jumper when she was teaching, and her head teacher asked her to remove it and she said, 'No' [...] I will always have an abiding memory [...] of her coming to a women-only disco that we ran above a rather grotty pub in Aberdeen, full of punky types, lesbians, women [...] and I thought bravo! [...] And she wrote us – myself and my sister – a letter, before she died, to be opened after she had died. And one of the things she said in the letter was that she had learned so many interesting things from the way I had lived my life [...] that she wouldn't have encountered at all as a primary school teacher in the far north of Scotland. But she'd heard about Greenham, she went to a women-only disco [...] she learned about Nicaragua, all these kinds of things. She met my friends and people that she wouldn't have otherwise met, so that was lovely.

This sense of a wider shared community of Greenham women often supported and influenced the futures of individuals in the movement. Like several of our interviewees, Sally Hay was inspired, after her time as an activist, to go into law and address the power imbalance that she had witnessed when working with others at the camp. Discussing the power the authorities had over the women during actions, she said:

This sort of standoff occurred [...] and ultimately they would win. They would get their lorry out, because they've got great big heavy lorries and a police force. And we've got a load of candles. And then, sometimes we would then quickly get into vehicles and follow them, and overtake them and stop in the road, and you know, and there was terrible – 'This is treason!' And [...] 'Obstructing Her Majesty's armaments!' There was all sorts of spurious legal twattery talk [...] And it was partly the absolute legal nonsense that was being spoken, that made me think, 'This is ridiculous.' And that's actually why I became a barrister [...] the police and bailiffs talk nonsense in legalese, and then win the day, and I felt, 'No, no, no!'

Sally did a conversion degree and converted her philosophy degree into a law one:

And then did the Bar straight afterwards [...] I really am a good middle-class girl. I was brought up by two doctors in the Midlands, you know, I went to a grammar school, you know, honestly, I am not an 'out-there terrorist'. And so I was really surprised to find that the police lied about people. I mean, honestly, it was a surprise. Now, obviously, after thirty years as a lawyer – it's absolutely par for the course, isn't it? I realised that it happens all the time [...] different reporting of the same events. I'm a great believer in, and all my clients at some point or other hear me saying, 'It's much more likely it was a cock-up than a conspiracy.' But there were out-and-out 'She swung a punch at me' situations, that, you know, I knew had not happened. I was there, I saw it [...]

I never saw a woman kick, punch or spit. And you know, the police statements said that women did that, and they didn't. They just didn't. I saw women swearing. I saw women blocking – you know, obstructing – if you want to charge people for obstruction, okay. There was a lot of obstruction going on. But I did not see women enacting violence on police officers, and I know that the statements that the police made in Newbury magistrates courts frequently said that they did [...] they were writing that 'I saw the lady I now recognise to be Miss Ann R Key [Greenham code: Miss Anarchy] throwing a punch at officer

So-and-So.' And no, she didn't [...] And that was one of the things that I thought, 'No, no, no, we need our own lawyers.'

Sally quickly realised that the Greenham women weren't the only ones in need of decent representation: 'Yeah, we need our own lawyers [...] and I maintain that we still do in relation to [...] victims of domestic violence [...] The homeless, the refugees – they need their own lawyers. They need people with an understanding of their situation who are coming from a position which is not to judge them before it starts.'

The personal was the political for Sally in several ways. When she started the Bar in 1989, she said: 'I think women were less than twenty per cent of barristers at that time [...] although not of the judiciary.' It was this predominately male environment that bred sexism which almost cost Sally her place in the progressive chambers on which she had set her sights. 'I had a terrible interview there,' she said. 'They were talking about how I have enormous boobs and good legs. And I also had a small child at the time, and this was the entire focus of the interview. I came out absolutely shattered.'

Not long afterwards, Sally bumped into a fellow Greenham woman on Hampstead Heath who was going out with a member of the chambers, whom she told about the experience. Later, Sally received a phone call:

Their head of chambers phoned me in my flat and said, 'We've reported ourselves to the Bar council, because we've had a meeting and realised that we've behaved in a way, in what is now called a sexist way towards you, and this is what's called discriminatory. And we are very sorry about it. So we have reported ourselves to the Bar council.' And I said, 'I'm perfectly well aware of what discrimination means. And, frankly, everybody else got twenty minutes on the law. And I got nineteen minutes on the size of my tits. I want twenty minutes on the law.' And he said, 'Tell me about the sexual discrimination legislation that's current at the moment.' And so I did, because I'd had a glass of wine and I was very cross, and we got to the end of it, and I said, 'So am I going to get my interview and my twenty minutes on the law?' And he said, 'You've got the tenancy.' And that was actually the start of my career.

Sally went on to provide free representation for Greenham women, South Africans protesting apartheid, and a variety of activists and human rights campaigners.

Annei Soanes agreed that Greenham had fed directly into her career and overarching life decisions. 'And here I am, much later on – all those years later, and all of my learning of that time has influenced the rest of my life,' she told us:

> And that philosophy around non-violence, that questioning, that recognition of the power of the human spirit, that sense of us being interdependent, but not co-dependent – what it means to have healthy relationships [...] existentialism, all of that stuff grew out of that time for me, actually laid the foundation for me to want to be a psychotherapist [...] What I hold now in my career, in my work as a psychotherapist, all of that actually – all the seeds of that came from that time in the peace movement at Greenham, as part of being in a women's group [...] I am eternally, eternally grateful and pleased that I was able to be part of something so profoundly important for women.

Also drawn to working as a therapist and healer, Sue Bolton felt her choices were a reaction to the emotional and physical impact of being an activist:

> So we did that huge concentrated momentum of energy that went on for – I don't know how many years it was, and then a lot of us got very ill. And I think you need to know that, a lot of us cracked up because you can't have that massive output of energy, emotional, mental, spiritual energy, and your kids, and not get ill [...] I heard, gradually over the years, that that happened to a lot of women, that they got ill [...] and it was like an opening of a door for them. So for me, I just went and hid, and then discovered meditation and yoga. A lot of us became therapists of different kinds, lots of us. So it was about going right back into yourself and realising that the whole thing starts from you, world peace doesn't come in a great big loud noise necessarily. It comes from a very quiet place within us. And then you change the

whole world, just by being yourself and finding out who you are. And we're very powerful in that way.

For many women, it seemed their personal journey into the political could also be made into the professional. With her role in the socialist folk music scene of the 1970s and 1980s, Frankie Armstrong was aware of the movement to set up and sustain Greenham:

I just thought the best thing I can do is help raise funds, kind of be a spokeswoman, or a singing spokesperson. So that's what I did [...] I was always back in touch at various events and workshops and concerts with women who were back and forth from Greenham [...] when I was touring in North America or Australia [...] I'd sing those songs and talk about Greenham, you know [...] I felt I could be a little bit of an ambassador for the British women's movement, but particularly Greenham.

Several of our interviewees had made their careers in the arts and media, often drawing on Greenham for inspiration, such as musicians Carolyn Francis, Jane Griffiths and Jill 'Ray' Raymond, theatre practitioners Illona Linthwaite and Penny Gulliver, writer Ann Pettitt, and journalist and textile artist Lyn Barlow.

Similarly inspired to share the impact of the Greenham sisterhood, Maggie Parks dedicated her working life to protecting women and challenging male violence. 'We had a Women for Life on Earth meeting in about 1987 at my flat,' Maggie told us:

And I can remember there were seventeen women in that room. And we suddenly started talking about childhood sexual abuse. And out of those seventeen women, twelve had experienced either childhood sexual abuse, rape or domestic violence. And it was out of that group, that the Women for Life on Earth group, that we started Worcester Rape Crisis Centre. So that was my move into working around violence against women. And, you know, that was directly influenced by everything I'd learned at Greenham, and about all the power structures, you know, that violence against women is a cause and a consequence of inequality.

Music is a huge part of the legacy of Greenham Common, with various copies of *The Greenham Songbook* being collated by the women over the years and providing the inspiration for the title and chapters of this book. (Sandie Hicks)

This was only the beginning of Maggie's work challenging our culture of male violence against women. Her next move was to Cornwall:

> I saw a poster saying that a helpline for rape and sexual abuse survivors was closing and that they wanted more women involved, and that was down in Redruth [...] so I went to that meeting, and I met a woman there called Val [...] and we just clicked [...] she was a wild woman, and she'd been to Greenham [...] She was doing an MA in Women's Studies, she took me to meet a whole group of women who were doing the Plymouth MA in Women's Studies, and round a kitchen table once again we set up the Women's Rape and Sexual Abuse Centre, from which the Women's Centre morphed [...] on the twentieth of March 2018 [...] So Val and I sort of were the founding members of the Women's Rape and Sexual Abuse Centre. And we've held that spirit of Greenham [...] and those ideas [...] the

sort of melding of eco-feminism and radical feminism, I think, really is at the heart of the organisation [...] And a lot of the work we do with women is very creative [...] we do body therapies here, we do lots of alternative therapies and we take women out in nature [...] And so I really do believe that [...] that energy is still held here in this little place in Cornwall, by a little nucleus of women who, you know, carried Greenham home and still carry it in their hearts really.

With a different Greenham friend, Maggie also created another legacy:

Vron and I started a women's writing magazine [...] there was a women's writing journal called *Woman Spirit* that two women in America, on the west coast of America, had edited for ten years. And in 1989, they'd done a ten-year cycle, and they decided to stop and we said, 'Oh, we're gonna miss it so much.' Vron said, 'Why don't we start our own?' So, again, out of Greenham, we started *From the Flames* [...]

Women were really beginning to understand how important myth and symbols were to them and how all our myths have been turned against us, and how all our symbols have been appropriated by the patriarchy [...] They'd burned thousands of us as witches, you know, the uncovering of women's her-story was really important to understand the mythologies that had been turned against us, and to rediscover our symbols.

So, for me it was it was a real melding of mind, body, spirit, [...] the excitement for me was about finding community. It was about finding like-minded women, but it was also this massive excitement of ideas and intellectual philosophies, because I think feminism is so exciting because it is ever-changing [...] It's moving, we called it *the* women's movement, but actually, it's women's movement. And it's been fascinating being in feminism for so long and seeing so many changes.

FROM THE FLAMES

'I remember having an insight (...) you've got to build, you can't just protest, you've got to build (...) you've got to build a future as well (...) you know, the positive as well as the negative, because it's very easy just to get negative (...) So that was one of the big things for me (...) about being at Greenham: I went away with a real clear sense of that (...) you can't just say, "This is no good." You've got to build what you think is good.'

Carolyn Francis

During the life of the camp, two major focuses of the women's campaigning would be resolved. Firstly, having seen the cruise missiles arrive, the women would also see their departure from the base and from UK soil. Secondly, a small group of women would stay on, working with Newbury locals to ensure the American military renounced its claim on Greenham Common and that the British government gave it back to the British people.

Judith Baron was living at camp when the cruise missiles started to leave. 'I was actually on breakfast television with Joan Ruddock [...] the day when they went,' she explained. 'It felt like we, you know, sort of achieved something [...] I feel there's always money for war [...] they'll spend billions and billions, and there's always money for that. But then, for things, you know, keeping people alive, or keeping people healthy, there isn't money, and I feel it's just totally twisted.'

Margaret McNeill, reflecting in her interview about Greenham's achievements, recalled a frequent criticism of the movement:

A lot later in life, I can remember a young person saying to me, 'Well, what was the point? What a waste.' I said, 'Well, we got rid of the bombs.' They said, 'No you didn't.' I said, 'Yeah, we did. Greenham women got rid of the bombs – they went.' They said, 'No, no, that was nothing to do with you.' I said, 'Do you honestly think that people's awareness would have been raised if the Greenham women hadn't been there? If all those women hadn't gone and been a thorn in the flesh of those people?'

Sue Lent agreed: 'We politicised a lot of people about the nuclear threat, and about nuclear weapons, about nuclear power.' Greenham, she pointed out, 'had a huge impact on raising people's awareness'. Sue Say was also emphatic about the Greenham women's campaigning impact:

I think that the publicity that came from that made it much easier for nuclear weapons to be shoved out. I think that if we hadn't been doing what we were doing, that would have just got so much worse – they would have started housing them all over the place [...] we highlighted it, and kept it in the news, and kept doing things to make sure it stayed in the news, in the minds of people.

Jill 'Ray' Raymond, who lived at camp on and off for most of its duration, remembered that, with the missiles leaving, the impression was given that work at Greenham was done: 'We were having visitors from Japan, and Australia, and America, and all across Europe, come to visit us, we were still having journalists from all over the world, but the word was – in the *Guardian*, all of them – was, "Oh they've gone home now, there's no more women there."' But in Ray's opinion, and to the minds of the women who stayed on mostly at Blue and Yellow Gates, the work was far from over.

With the British government shifting its attention from cruise to Trident, and the Iraq war looming, it seemed more important than ever not to give up on getting Greenham Common itself away from the military:

The story was that it was a USAFA [United States Air Force Academy] base with a temporary fence around the common for the Second World War, and the US had gone home, but the fence had never come down. And our air force stayed there [...] So actually it was about reclaiming the land and reclaiming the common, and that's why a lot of women stayed even though the missiles had gone home – because the fence was still there. And the first, you know, really big actions were about pulling the fence down, because we wanted to see the back of the fence, and we wanted to reclaim the common.

With the camp numbers reduced and the remaining women focused on a local goal, the movement to 'Reclaim the Common' actually healed some of the wounds between the women and the locals. Some residents of the nearby towns joined the women's campaign, standing up for them in the community and the local press. A letter with the title 'MoD More Guilty Than Greenham Women' was printed in a Newbury paper from a Berkshire farmer, and reveals the shifting political allegiances:

15 August 1991

I was very surprised to read the outburst from Wing Commander Brookes in last week's paper. The supposed bad behaviour and waste of the 'harridans' pales into insignificance when compared to that of the Ministry of Defence.

Who was it who purchased the land after threats of compulsory purchase? Who was it who forcibly evicted the commoners and the public with a 12-foot fence and guard dogs? Who was it who built hundreds of millions of pounds' worth of structures illegally on our common? Who was it who purported to have extinguished commoners' rights without testing their case in courts of law? The answer of course is the organisation charged with protecting the rights and freedoms of the British people.

If the MoD had any confidence in the validity of their case they would not have opposed the application by Commons Against for a judicial review of their right to extinguish commoners' rights.[24] They would also have had a public enquiry as promised by the government in 1958 before any land was expropriated by the MoD. They would also have applied to the Department of the Environment for permission to erect their buildings and to revoke rights of public access to Crookham Common.[25] Instead we have unproved claims and a steamroller driven over the requirements of the law.

These are the sort of official tactics one would associated with the governments of Eastern Europe, the ones who were told by Mrs Thatcher that the 'rule of law is paramount'. So, Wing Commander Brookes, put your own house in order before you carp on about the petty misdemeanours of the peace women. When they have gone to court recently, they have been vindicated.[26]

Lynette Edwells told us about the Commons Again group 'that successfully fought to restore Greenham Common to the people' and was headed by 'Wendy and Leslie Pope, Newbury members of Newbury Campaign against Cruise Missiles, Cruisewatchers and supporters of the peace camp'. Wendy, like her friend Lynette, had supported the camp throughout its life on the common, opening her home for Greenham women's friends and family to stay. Leslie was influential in advising women on the dole that they could claim for heating and lighting benefits as well, 'which they did,' Lynette noted gleefully, 'infuriating the RAGE [Ratepayers Against the Greenham Encampments] group that was campaigning for benefits to the Peace Women to be stopped'.

It is thanks to the continued determination of the Greenham women who stayed on at camp after cruise left, and the united efforts they co-ordinated with the local population, that visitors to Greenham Common today can enjoy the green space that has been rightfully returned to them as British citizens. The military buildings have been repurposed in a number of ways to serve the community, including museums, exhibition spaces, cafes, arts hubs and, as Lorna Richardson gleefully related to us in her interview, the site of the rebel base for the Star Wars film *The Force Awakens*. Sitting with her son in the cinema, Lorna 'thought [she] would just combust with joy' when she realised 'there was Leia running the resistance from Greenham [...] and I'm like "Oh my god, I've died and gone to heaven!"'

The women didn't leave political campaigning when they left the camp. Throughout the interviews, accounts of further activism are aplenty. Lorna related:

It was because of Greenham that I became involved in the Namibia support committee and going to Namibia, and working with Southern

African activists was one of the formative experiences of my life. And I came to that because the British nuclear weapons programme was using uranium that was being taken [...] from Namibian uranium mines, which had huge problems for Namibian miners and, you know, apartheid was in full swing and Namibia were occupied by the South African apartheid state.

Likewise, Ray described 'A massive, massive network [...] another Greenham offshoot, and a separate project in its own right [...] Women's Aid for Former Yugoslavia', which was 'a huge Greenham network, outreach thing during the war in former Yugoslavia'. She told us:

> We were already connected to Women in Black in Serbia and Croatia, Zagreb and Belgrade, so we worked with them [...] There's a difference between displaced people and refugees in terms of who gets aid from the UN. So if you're a displaced person you don't qualify for aid, so we particularly worked through our sister organisations to support women, women and children, who were not getting UN aid [...] We worked with the Women's Institute, we worked with the Girl Guides, we had different campaigns. We did dozens of convoys, and I went three times [...] We hired trucks, and we took requested aid [...]
>
> There were Muslim and Christian women working together in a town in Krajina, which was a very contested area. And they'd salvaged out a bombed building to make a day centre for women, they got a washing machine – because it was very hard to get the washing done – so we supported them with soap powders [...] We had a knicker project one time to take knickers and sanitary stuff and nappies, and we supported [...] a medical centre [...] in Bosnia – so we took a lot of medicines out there, and also delivered training: rape crisis training, trauma training [...] And then also another project that came out of it was the Sock Project, so women who were in refugee camps [...] we'd take wool to them and they would knit their traditional socks, and we'd bring the socks back and sell them through independent bookshops to help raise funds.

Ray remembered 'driving through a war zone, you know, there was no traffic except military traffic. There were military road blocks and you couldn't get out and have a piss in the bush because of landmines [...] I had to go through Hungary to get to Serbia – they shut the customs points overnight, so we had to sleep in the tucks with three miles of Russian trucks waiting to come into Serbia in the morning!'

Several women we interviewed still go once a month to Aldermaston Women's Peace Camp where campaigns draw attention to nuclear weapons still being made there, and, during the Iraq war, highlighted the use of depleted uranium bombs by the USA. According to Ray, at that time women from Aldermaston 'were monitoring the depleted uranium that was being blown over Europe and in the UK from the stuff that was dropped by those weapons'.

Challenges to establishment, industry and big business feature regularly in the women's campaigns. Carolyn Francis has contributed to anti-fracking campaigns, and Sarah Green plays an important role in Stop HS2, the national campaign against High Speed 2, the new railway that is believed to threaten wildlife and safe drinking water in the south-east of England. Elizabeth Beech has been involved with Rise Up, Occupy and, like many of our interviewees, Extinction Rebellion. At the time of her interview, she hailed Extinction Rebellion as 'doing extremely well' at the difficult job of maintaining non-violence at mixed-sex protests and events. 'I'm very impressed with them,' she told us:

> That's the only group I've come across since Greenham who have a truly dedicated element to them about non-violence, and really want to explore it as a topic [...] I went on their first thing in Parliament Square [...] They give people really clear pieces of paper saying, 'Be friendly with policemen, they're people too, and they're being affected by climate change. There's no need to be shouting at people'. They really do keep a very tight ship on it.

The successful lawsuit that Sue Say and her fellow Greenham woman friend Stella developed against the MoD around the conducting of strip-searches benefitted not only women in prison, but also women going through immigration processes or being deported:

What came out of Greenham that will be forever changed is the way that the Ministry of Defence, and immigration, and police officers [...] treat human beings when entering and leaving their facilities. They now have to be a damn sight more careful than they ever used to have to be [...] There's been loads of cases that have spun off from that once we won ours [...] there's a few prisons that had a bit of a wake-up call as a result of that precedent being set.

Sue was also a regular on feminist marches which called for it to be illegal for a husband to rape his wife; thanks to the campaigns of feminists like Sue, this legislation was finally introduced in 1994.[27]

Janet Smith emphasised how 'Greenham women got involved in the Women in Prison movement' and she mentioned their involvement in 'Rape Crisis [...] in all kinds of different areas'. Janet mused that the camp was 'responsible for a whole generation of women who changed the way women behaved, I think [...] it showed what power women can have when they actually get together, and trust each other, and do things'. Janet felt that 'Greenham gave me a confidence [...] it's given me a physical confidence, or a way of handling myself, which I don't think I would have had. And the women's movement gave me sort of psychological confidence, really.'

She described being on a demonstration organised by her university against the Iraq war where she 'grabbed hold of a couple of my friends who are much younger, but kind of on-board, and said, "Let's sit down" and some people were horrified, but enough people sat down for there to be a blockade'. After a while, she recalled, the police 'picked us up and threw us, or certainly they threw me, because I remember a group of Asian lads got really indignant that they'd thrown a woman on the pavement'. But this didn't change the revelatory nature of the experience for Janet's friends, who said to her afterwards: 'I didn't think I'd have the courage to do that!'

Sue Lent agreed that Greenham had given women more courage to act or speak out publicly:

I think a lot of the Greenham women found themselves thrust out there, where you had to speak, you had to go to meetings and talk about what was happening. And, you kind of just had to do it [...] Because there was so many requests, really. And I'm not sure that I would have had the confidence to stand for the council if I hadn't been through that [...] I think for a lot of women in politics, it gave them more confidence, and it definitely did with me.

Sue was convinced that some of the positive changes she'd seen in politics in Wales had connections with women from Greenham. She described the time when she was first running for council:

There is still a great under representation of women in politics, but it has changed a lot. I mean, when I was first on the council in '89, on the Old South Glamorgan, in the Labour group, I think there was seven women out of about forty-six people and nobody really thought much of it. I mean, you know, it's not perfect now, I think we're about a third women [...] But it's still a big improvement and at least people do recognise that there should be equal representation. I mean, then people didn't really think about it. And I think some of the people that did think about it probably thought it wasn't very ladylike to be involved in politics, because of the macho style of politics [...] People say, 'I don't know how you can be involved in all that' as if it's sort of dirty or something. But, if we're not involved in political life, and stand for council, and as MPs, somebody else is going to fill the gap who hasn't got as much principle, or isn't prepared to fight for different things.

When asked if she felt Greenham had made an impact on women moving into these roles, she replied:

Somebody like Helen John dedicated their whole life to peace. And became well known and spoke at lots of events, and did a lot [...] There are an awful lot of women who were involved in Greenham who've gone on to it [...] Jane Hutt, who is a cabinet member in the Welsh Assembly, has virtually been a cabinet member right from its inception, she spoke before the original march set off. She was a South Glamorgan councillor [...] when she was first a councillor, there was probably only about two women on the council [...] another woman

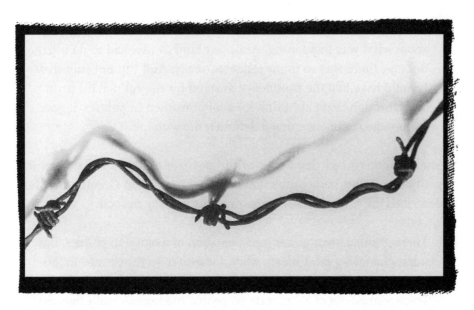

Many of the women took sections of the fence from Greenham away with them. (Bridget Boudewijn)

Fence-cutting souvenirs. (Penny Wilson)

went on to be an MP [...] even women like Glenys Kinnock, she spent
a lot of time going down to Greenham [...] I think it did spur people
on, and it did give us a certain amount of confidence, definitely.

The idea that Greenham increased women's confidence in public roles
was reinforced by Sue Say: 'I think the thing for me is there's that phrase
"Greenham women are everywhere". And any woman who can say that
we're everywhere understands the concept [...] It wasn't just about you
being in the dirt in that moment, it was also about the women who went
and did speeches.'

Never was that confidence more needed than when Sue found herself
speaking at a European conference: 'I was standing around at the camp
one day and somebody said, "Oh, you know, you haven't been on a talk
have you?" And I went, "What do you mean a talk?" "Oh, it's like there's
a women's group in Italy, and they want somebody to go and have a
little chat," and I thought, "Oh okay, I don't mind that – I've never been
abroad" [...] So I go with this separatist woman.'

Once there, Sue said of her initial impressions:

So we come into this room that was probably about twenty feet across.
And it had rows of seating [...] I'm thinking this is a bit of an odd place
to have a women's meeting.

Anyway, we come in and the woman I'm supposed to be speaking
with goes, 'Oh, no, there's men here, I'm not doing this.' Buggers
off and leaves me in this thing, and I'm thinking, what the hell is
this? Anyway, I'm looking at this guy and I'm thinking [...] that's really
weird, that man looks just like Kofi Annan. And this woman comes
over and goes, 'You're the second speaker, you'll just be introduced.'
I'm like, 'What, sorry?' [...] Then ping, ping, ping, ping, ping, ping
all these lights lighting up – rows and rows and rows. It was only the
European Peace Conference, and nobody had bothered to tell me that!

They told me I was going to be speaking to a women's group. And
there I was having to stand up in front of 270,000 people [...] It was
the International Peace Conference, and I was on the platform with
Kofi Annan. Anyway, Kofi Annan then goes up after me, and he's like,
'What a fantastic speaker. I'd like to pay tribute to the last speaker.'

And I'm like thinking, that is Kofi Annan [...] one of those sort of moments where you think, 'I don't think this has happened.'

WOMAN TIGER, WOMAN DOVE

In the women's accounts, we see the chance the camp gave for its occupants to get to know themselves, their strengths and weaknesses, outside of their roles as 'good' mothers, partners or daughters. Additionally, we see the opportunities that arose for them to hone their voice and widen their horizons beyond those offered by family, husbands, boyfriends and conventional jobs. Janet Smith told us:

> I've never particularly looked for the protection of men, or expected it. I think it's more about having confidence in your own power and knowing who you are, and a lot of women don't know who they are. It's just like something that's missing in the curriculum [...] And I still think although things have changed a lot, they haven't changed anywhere near as much as we think they have. And I think there's a danger of them sort of going backwards, really.

Discussions about the push and pull of progress and oppression came up time and again. Annei Soanes echoed Janet's fears of a backslide for women's rights: 'Women are still being exploited in lots of different ways. Women are still being put down, women's voices are still being silenced.' Sue Lent noted that when she was getting ready to march to Greenham, laws like the 'Sex Discrimination Act [...] and the Equal Pay Act, they hadn't been in very long then', and 'women were treated differently' in ways that today 'young women tend to take more for granted'. Judith Baron feared feminist heritage was not accessible to the next generations:

> We had an LGBT awareness session at work, this was a few years ago. And our manager, he was saying, 'Oh were any of you at Greenham?'

But a lot of the younger women in their twenties had never heard of it. So I think it's good that you're doing this [...] Because at the time it was such a big thing, that whether people agreed with it or didn't, everyone knew Greenham Common. And now it's just like, it's sort of disappeared [...] I don't think people realise how massive it was at the time [...] even if it was negative there was something in the paper virtually every day about Greenham.

Similarly, Becky Griffiths ruminated on the difference between how Suffrage history has now been commemorated while Greenham has been largely erased:

I wonder if it was because [...] one of the things that women were asking for in the Suffrage movement was so establishment, you know – we want to be able to vote, we want to be able to vote in your system that you've made. So all we want to do is join your system [...] And I think the Greenham women's kind of movement was not that at all. We didn't want that system [...] we weren't interested in those rules. And so I think maybe it's a harder thing to quantify. And the success of it is probably harder to quantify as well, you know, you campaign for the vote, you get the vote. That's how that's measured. You campaign for an anti-nuclear world, or for peace [...] that's harder to measure [...] So maybe that's why [...] I think it's probably a mixture of those things. We wanted something wilder, we wanted something less easy to measure.

Alison Napier acknowledged the different challenges that women would face today in terms of creating something like Greenham:

What's happened in the last twenty plus years has trapped an awful lot of people into not feeling they can step out of their lives to do something about their planet. Even things like I was able to sign on and go away for two or three weeks – you used to be able to sign on and then take a holiday from signing on, so you could miss signing on for a fortnight, so you could go away for a month. Today you can't do that. You have to show that you have applied for seventeen jobs every three days. If you don't you get sanctioned, and then you lose your money, and then you lose your home [...]

I think at the time we were going to Greenham, it was easier to step out. I was a student for a while, but I didn't have a student debt [...] we got a grant, we got our fees paid, it was easier to do something different. And then you would rent somewhere to live and you would get housing benefit, and nobody would say, 'Oh get your foot on the property ladder, quick.' You know, people in their twenties have got mortgages, and I think a mortgage is one of the greatest tools of social control that there is [...] That's housing policy [...] you could say that housing policy in the United Kingdom has dictated who is able to protest, because you can't rent affordably and securely, it's not an option any more [...] Everything is linked [...] One of the symbols of Greenham was the spider's web, and it's all linked. Welfare rights, benefit systems, housing, it's all linked. Student debts – it's all linked.

But while acknowledging today's challenges, many of our Greenham women interviewees were keen to raise awareness of the need for protest in people's lives now. 'What was important for me about Greenham was the fact that it was like the best education you'll ever have,' Sue Say explained:

Because you do not very often in life get an opportunity to sit side by side with someone very different to yourself. We all sort of migrate to people who are like us, or who do things like us. We naturally do that [...] Greenham was about sitting next to someone with your arm linked to them, grounding yourself to stop the disaster from happening. I didn't care whether this woman was an accountant, or a lawyer, or a solicitor, or a nurse, or a teacher. It didn't matter to me what colour she was, what country she was from, what religion she had. It was the fact that we were here united as women. And we were going to change the world. We were going to stop this oppression from happening [...] We were going to peacefully say, 'No'.

And that was the point – it was about women working in peace, to say, 'No'. It wasn't about aggression or violence. It was about women linking arms with each other, sitting in the dirt, refusing to move [...] And it was questioning the authority, making the police react, making them have to see and justify and acknowledge what they were doing [...] I think the fact that we as a bunch of disorganised individuals – you know, we were not a united front! We all did things so very differently. And that was the beauty of it, you can't fight something that comes at you in so many different ways.

Alongside the revelations and achievements, each wave of feminism brings debates within the movement: issues like the sex industry and the definition of gender are setting sister against sister at the time of writing. Sue's analysis on the importance of women campaigning together also spoke to what might heal and unify the movement for the liberation of women and girls going forward:

For me, that working together thing, knowing we were all different, knowing that a woman probably would stand up and argue with me for half an hour on one tiny little thing because we don't agree, but she will sit here and link arms with me, and make sure that we stop nuclear weapons, is all that I needed to hear. And I think for me, that is how Greenham women are everywhere.

That's what I took with me, and I took that understanding that all women are different. And that somebody's opposing view to mine, they have just as much right to express it. And I need to hear, I need to listen. And if she's wrong, in my view, I need to persuade her. And if I'm wrong, she needs to persuade me. She needs to enlighten me, and I need to enlighten her. That's both our responsibilities. So it is the responsibility of those at Greenham to share that.

I've told as many Greenham stories as I can my whole life, because for me, they form who I am. They made me see the things that I will accept, and the things that I will not. They taught me lines that I will cross, and lines that I will not. I will never refuse a woman water or food, I will not do that. I will never step over that line. And that's a line that I don't think any real Greenham woman would.

Alison seconded this need for collective action:

It's important because everyone, but particularly women, but every-one, has to understand that you can affect change in your world. And it's important because I think the world now [...] is in a desperately bad way [...] I don't think wise people's voices are heard so much now, and they have to be. And I would love young people to believe that they can step out of the terribly narrow tram-lines that their lives get channelled into. And it doesn't matter what some influencer on Instagram says they should be wearing or doing to their nails this week [...] image doesn't matter.

Alison felt strongly that 'to step away from that and to believe that *you* can influence and make a difference' was what was vital:

But the stage before that is to see that a difference has to be made, because I think there's not much – in the mainstream media certainly – that even would suggest that there's that much wrong. There, in slightly smaller print: 'Oh, another rainforest has gone, or another war has started, or another tens of thousands of refugees have ended up somewhere where nobody wants them there either' [...] It's the contradiction between suddenly everybody is so connected, but nobody is really touching each other [...]

This interview could go round the world in two seconds if you wanted it to, and then in another five minutes' time another one would have gone round the world [...] Everything is desperately important for four seconds, I think that's my sense. And then the next desperately important thing is desperately important for four seconds, and on it goes. And I think Greenham made time for people to speak to each other, and to explore their own ideas, and to take their ideas back to their communities to do with them what they would.

Greenham Common Women's Peace Camp emerged from our interviewees' testimonies as a piece of history that was vital to be shared and learned from, to enable women and to connect them. To connect them with each other and to connect them with their sense of self, of sisterhood, of responsibility, of power. 'I think it not only honours what it means to be a woman in the world,' Margaret McNeill said:

It represents the questioning of ourselves, of society, of the world in general. The personal is the political [...] I think as human beings, we always need to question that. Who am I as a person living in the world? What do I contribute? How do I impact? What do I need? How can we build a better world, a better future for generations that follow us? [...] Women's history [...] is always forgotten. So it feels important to remember this [...]

It reflects my sense of at the time, I want my name [...] on that list of people that says, 'I do not think nuclear weapons is the right way to go' [...] It's putting my name to this invisible charter that says, 'I was there, I witnessed this, this is important.' Because we're all responsible in this world for contributing, we're all responsible for ourselves. And to some extent, we're all responsible for other people. We have to make ourselves accountable. We share this world.

Reflecting on a life of campaigning that started at Greenham, Lorna Richardson said: 'I have been very fortunate in that I have been part of political movements which won and so I'm quite cheerful about a lot of things – and I'm absolutely bloody terrified at a whole bunch more.' Having experienced both the elation and camaraderie of victory, and also the fear that knowledge, compassion and empathy make inevitable, Lorna summed up her views on Greenham:

A lot of women's work is rendered invisible, because people think that elves did it, in the night, it happened magically with no actual input involved. And the thing about a lot of Greenham is that we did it on tuppence. It was women with no money, no time [...] I mean, Rebecca, you were talking about your mum? She had you. Women were carving time out of their lives that they did not have to spare. They were carving money out of their lives that they did not have to spare, they were carving emotional energy out of their lives that they did not have to spare. And all those women created something that changed things, it changed public policy at a national level [...]

I mean, Britain didn't go unilateralist and is unlikely to do anytime soon. But you create the conditions in which people make decisions in a different way than they would have before. And it changed the international situation as part of a larger whole. And it changed individual women to a massive extent, some of whom have then gone on to create other things. It changed a way of working; the way I learned to work at Greenham, that collaborative way, has shaped my entire life. I believe it's done the same for a lot of other women.

All those things took women who did not have the time, who did not have the money, who did not have the energy, and who did it anyway. To have, you know, the idea that all that political movement would have happened without that work, it's not true. And so, that's why I am grateful for any initiative that records it, partly because, well, partly because elves didn't do it in the night. We did it. I did it, your mum did it. Loads of other women did it.

As the Greenham women tell us, 'We are the flow, we are the ebb, we are the weaver, we are the web'. It is a reminder that there are waves of action needed, and that we can both create and be change. Their campaign inspires and their words invoke the need for sisterhood. They remind us that the time is now.

Frankie: It's lovely to still have these connections still, you know.
Interviewer: The web is intact.
Frankie: It is. It is. Which is pretty exciting. And you know, we're not going to live forever, for heaven's sake, you know, quite a lot of us are in our seventies or eighties. So, you know, over to you lovely women. But it's true isn't it?
Interviewer: Yeah, it is. And over to the people listening to this as well, you know? Hopefully. For time immemorial.
Frankie: And they'll be in the different parts of the world too. It's got to be an international movement.
Interviewer: And it's all of our responsibility, isn't it?
Frankie: Yeah.[28]

One of the most prolific Greenham badges. Women put this sign in toilets along motorways; they shocked friends, family and colleagues by wearing it. It was a show of solidarity, a message that Greenham women couldn't be defined or dismissed. They were a sisterhood that was, and is, everywhere. (Jenny Engledow)

NOTES

1   UK Parliament, *EDM 832: De-activation of Greenham Common*; Historic England, *Cruise Missile Shelter Complex, Greenham Common Airbase*; *The Guardian*, 'Cruise Missiles Leave Greenham (1989 to 2000)', 03/05/2007.

2   www.greenhamwpc.org.uk.

3   Federation of American Scientists, *RT-21M / SS-20 Saber*.

4   *The Guardian*, 'Death of the Treaty that Removed Missiles from Greenham Common', 01/08/2019.

5   Smithsonian, Air and Space Museum, *Pershing II*.

6   Arms Control Association, *U.S. Completes INF Treaty Withdrawal*.

7   *The Intercept*, 'Inside Menwith Hill', 06/09/2016.

8   Anti-War Songs, *The Greenham Songbook*.

9   UK Parliament, *1928 Equal Franchise Act*.

10 UK Parliament, House of Commons Library, *The History and Geography of Women MPs Since 1918 in Numbers*.

11 Legislation UK, *Criminal Justice and Public Order Act 1994*.

12 *The Guardian*, 'The Day that Feminists Took "Women's Lib" to the Streets', 03/03/2018; People's History of the NHS, *Birth Control and the Contraceptive Pill on the NHS*; Legislation UK, *Sex Discrimination Act 1975*; Legislation UK, *Domestic Violence and Matrimonial Proceedings Act 1976*; Margaret Thatcher Foundation, *Guide to the Archives, 1979–1990*.

13 British Social Attitudes, *Gender Roles: A Generational Shift in Attitudes?*

14 An international arts festival – World of Music, Arts and Dance.

15 *On History*, 'Women and Peace: Pat Arrowsmith and Greenham Common', 06/05/2019.

16 A reference to Scud missiles, used by British forces in the Falklands War.

17 BBC News, 'On This Day, 2nd May 1982'.

18 Lib Quotes: Einstein, Albert, *Einstein's 1912 Manuscript on the Special Theory of Relativity*, ed. George Braziller, 2003.

19 *Wales Online*, 'The Woman Who Paid the Ultimate Price for Peace', 04/09/2013.
20 *Berkshire Live*, 'Looking Back at the Hungerford Massacre 33 Years On', 19/08/2020.
21 BBC News, 'Colin Campbell Sentenced to Life for Claire Woolterton 1981 Murder', 04/12/2013.
22 *Peace Magazine*, 'Zapping the Movement', 01/06/1987.
23 Justia, *Greenham Women Against Cruise Missiles v. Reagan, 591 F. Supp. 1332 (S.D.N.Y. 1984)*.
24 A support group that aided those commoners who were against the expropriation of the land.
25 The RAF base straddled Crookham Common and Greenham Common.
26 Letter supplied by Jill 'Ray' Raymond, from her private archive.
27 Legislation UK, *Criminal Justice and Public Order Act 1994*.
28 From Frankie Armstrong's interview in the Greenham Women Everywhere archive.

BIBLIOGRAPHY

BOOKS

Baron, Judith, *Greenham Common Women's Peace Camp 1985–1994* (UK: self-published, 2021)

Chezar, Oak, *Trespassing: A Memoir of Greenham Common* (USA: Indy Pub, 2020)

Cook, Alice and Kirk, Gwyn, *Greenham Women Everywhere: Dreams, Ideas and Actions from the Women's Peace Movement* (London: Pluto Press, 1983)

Davies, Stephanie, *Other Girls Like Me* (California: Bink Books, 2020)

Harford, Barbara and Hopkins, Sarah (eds), *Greenham Common: Women at the Wire* (London: The Women's Press, 1984)

Pettitt, Ann, *Walking to Greenham: How the Peace-Camp Began and the Cold War Ended* (South Glamorgan: Honno, 2006)

Roseneil, Sasha, *Common Women, Uncommon Practices: The Queer Feminisms of Greenham* (London: Cassell & Co., 2000)

Roseneil, Sasha, *Disarming Patriarchy: Feminism and Political Action at Greenham* (Buckingham: Open University Press, 1995)

WEBSITES

Anti-War Songs:
    www.antiwarsongs.org
Greenham Women Digital:
    www.greenhamwomen.digital
The Greenham Women Everywhere Archive:
    www.greenhamwomeneverywhere.co.uk
The Heroine Collective:
    www.theheroinecollective.com

'Orange Gate Journal: A Personal View of the Greenham Common
    Women's Peace Camp', by Ginette Leach:
        www.orangegatejournal.co.uk
Scary Little Girls, Greenham Game:
        www.scarylittlegirls.co.uk/campfire

ARCHIVES

The Greenham/Lynette Edwell Archive, at the Berkshire Record Office
The Women's Library, Greenham Archive, at the London School
    of Economics

THANK YOUS

We want to express our gratitude to the web of people who have made this book possible. We have aimed to simply be conduits for the many testimonies and varied archival materials that have been so generously shared with us on the Greenham Women Everywhere archive, that we may help preserve and disseminate this important history. Thank you to everyone who helped us do that with their time, talent, energy and commitment.

Thank you to Laura Perehinec and all at The History Press for making this book possible.

To all the Greenham women who shared their stories with us, we thank you and all the thousands of women who came together to make the world a better place:

Ailsa Johnson; Alison Napier; Angela Akehurst; Ann and Sally Bell; Ann Pettitt; Ann Scargill; Anna and Mary Birch; Annei Soanes; Anni Tracy; Annie Brotherton; Atalanta Kernick; Becky Barnes; Becky Griffiths; Betty Cook; Betty Levene; Bridget Boudewijn; Caroline Poland; Carolyn Francis; Catherine Leyow; Celia Chasey; Claire Pattinson; Clayre Gribben; Diana Derioz; Diana Proudfoot; Janet Smith; Elizabeth Beech; Elizabeth Greenland; Elizabeth Woodcraft; Elspeth Owen; Evelyn Parker; Fenja Hill; Fran De'Eath; Frankie Armstrong; Gerd Browne; Gillian Booth; Hannah Schafer; Hazel Pegg; Heather Platt; Helen Garland; Helen MacRae; Helen Moore; Helen Steel; Helena Nightingale; Hilary Gould; Hilary Whyard; Hoonie Feltham; Illona Linthwaite; Jade Britton; Jan; Jane Griffiths; Janice Candler; Jeanne Diamond; Jenny Craigen; Jenny Engledow; Jill 'Ray' Raymond; Joanna Mattingly; Josetta Malcolm; Jude Munden; Judith Baron; Judith Niechcial; Judy Harris; Julia Ball; Karen Fisher; Karmen Thomas; Kate Whittle; Kathy Trevelyan; Leah Thalman; Lisa Halse; Lorna Richardson; Louella Crisfield; Lyn Barlow; Lynette Edwell; Lynne Wilkes; Maggie Parks; Margaret McNeill; Maria Ragusa; Mary Woodvine; Mercedes Kemp; Mica May;

Muswell Hill Women; Nina Millns; Padmarajni Ann Ward; Peggy Seeger; Penny Gane; Penny Gulliver; Pixie Taylor; Polly High; Rosalind Clark; Rosemary Jarrett Nottingham; Rosy Bremer; Ruth Nichol; Sally Hay; Sarah Green; Sarah Hopkins; Sheila Eschle; Sheila Thornton; Silver Moon; Southampton and Eastleigh Women; Margaret Kenyon, now Maggie O'Connor, et al. (Jean Karlsen, Vicki Orba, Hazel Bingham, Ingrid Peckham and Jo Crook); Stephanie Davies; Sue Bolton; Sue Lent; Sue Say; Suzanne Novak; Tamsin Clayton; Tanya Myers; Tarn Lamb; Vicki Smith; Voz Faragher; Wendy Daniels; Wendy Johns; Zohl de Ishtar.

Thank you to the interviewers, who engaged and empathised so much in each conversation they had with the Greenham women:

Alice Robinson; Christine Bradshaw; Elaine Ruth White; Emily Strange; Emma Gliddon; Florence Weston; Isabelle Tracy; Jessica Leyton; Josephine Liptrott; June Hughes; Kitty Gurnos Davies; Leslie Lyle; Nicky Arikoglu; Jill 'Ray' Raymond; Sara Sherwood; Sarah Learmonth; Tricia Grace Norton.

Thank you to all our artists and archivists for their photographs and images:

Bridget Boudewijn; Christine Bradshaw; Dawn Stewart; Gini Mags; Illona Linthwaite; Janet Smith; Jenny Engledow; Jude Munden; Linda Broughton; LSE Women's Library Archives.; Lyn Barlow; Paula Allen; Penny Wilson; Sandie Hicks on behalf of the Exeter Peace Women; Sarah Booker; Sue Lent.

Thank you to those who gave invaluable insights and project support:

Becky Barry; Becky John; Chris Morris; Clare Johnson; Finn Mackay; Helen John; Lorna Partington; Rachael Miles; Rebecca Johnson; Sharon Foster.

Thank you to those who gave such care and attention to helping us prepare this book:

Adrian Walker; Tom Nash; Vanessa Pini.

Thank you to the Heritage Lottery Fund South West for making the archive possible.

Thank you to all our project partners who also helped make the archive possible:

Cornwall Council; Dreadnought South West; Falmouth University; Goldsmiths University of London; Kresen Kernow; the East End Women's Museum; the Feminist Library; the Hypatia Trust; the UK Parliament Vote 100 Project; the University of the West of England in Bristol; the Women's Library at the London School of Economics.

Rebecca would like to thank those who travelled the full journey with her, and those who didn't leave her emotional side while we got this thing done. She is very glad of you:

Steggy; Papa Noel; Dek; BeckySan; Jules; Maddog; Peaches; Shazz; and Gilbert Blyth Mordan.

And Kate would like to thank:

Glyn, Deborah and Amber for their love and support during the writing of this book, and love and thanks always to June, Alan, Tom and, of course, Finn Juno.